WHISPERS
OF THE HEART

Visionary Insight
PRESS

WHISPERS

OF THE HEART

WHISPERS OF THE HEART

ISBN: 978-0-9961389-0-1

The authors of this book do not dispense medical advice or prescribe the use of any technique as a form of treatment for physical or medical problems without the advice of a physician, either directly, or indirectly. If the reader chooses to use any of the information in this book, the author and publisher assume no responsibility for their actions.

Ordering information: Quantity Sales. Special discounts are available on quantity purchases by corporations, associations, and others. For details, contact the Special Sales Department at Visionary Insight Press.

Visionary Insight Press, 822 Westchester Place, Charleston, IL 61920

Visionary Insight Press, the Visionary Insight Press logo and its individual parts are trademarks of Visionary Insight Press.

Compiled by: Lisa Hardwick
Editor-At-Large: Chelle Thompson

Back cover photo credit: Jase White, Duygu Ozen of Moments Photography Studio, Paige Rudolph, Paula D. Moore, Rick Pickford, Courtney Munson – Coco Photography, Patricia Holdsworth Photography – Regina, Sask. Canada, Lifetouch, Stephanie Michelle Photography, Susan Sabo Photography, Long Beach, CA., Guy Viau, Brenda Cassidy Bailey, Toby Long, Edinburgh, Kaydin Carlsen of Santa Cruz, CA, Photographer Extraordinaire – Ernie Espejo, NCL Photographer, Simon Forder – The Castle Guy, Meggan Romphf, Cori Roberts Photography, Melissa Corter, Ryan Jay of Ryan Jay Photo

Courage is what it takes to stand
up and speak; courage is also what
it takes to sit down and listen.

~ WINSTON CHURCHILL

Table of Contents

Foreword

by Dr. Janice Marie Collins

Whispers *of the Heart* is a beautifully written book that imparts knowledge from the authentic locations of real-life experiences and ethereal awakenings. Twenty-nine talented and insightful authors, unselfishly, share their stories of finding hope, joy and love from courageous journeys they chose to take, or was chosen for them. Although some of the stories have elements of pain and strife, **all** of the stories provide gentle guidance, advice and support of a better day. In addition to having the important elements found in effective storytelling, the anecdotes offer a measure of hope to each reader. Each author offers something special to your knowledge base of spiritual growth. There is a story for everyone and each story will speak to your soul and spirit, personally, making it almost impossible for you not to be moved.

Angela N. Holton says that from birth you are on a Divine pathway to understanding Love and the role you play in creating pockets of Love to share with the world. You were born with the map located inside of you. You need only hear the *whispers from your heart* and obey. **Debbie Ledford** speaks of the euphoric feeling one has when connecting to and recognizing your inner voice. Stop, Look and Listen offers the time and silence needed to connect to the wisdom that is there just for you. **Tonya Thomas** has faced violence and threats to her own life, but, she is a survivor and teaches us how not to be afraid of the "Unknown." Simply believe. Part of believing means to open your "Third Eye," encouraged by

Michelle Mullady, who wants you to "see who you truly are." Michelle is an incredible spiritual teacher and you won't want to miss the guidance she has to share. **Gilly Kennedy** shares a special whisper just for you as she encourages us to continue living for the day when the light will dawn and **Halina Kurowska** says don't be afraid to take the "detour." You'll be surprised at what you may find. **Michele Hatfield Quesenberry** shows us how the trickery of self-preservation can overtake our *healthy intuition* and better judgment. Refocus. Life is about choices according to **Deanna Leigh**. Create them, lay them down on a map toward your goal and begin your journey, one step at a time. While you're on this journey, listen to both your head AND your heart. Together, they make an awesome team says **Carole Cassell**. Speaking of the heart, **Cheryl Guttenberg** takes a Maya Angelou passage to heart when she writes about asking, "for what you want and be prepared to get it." How many times have we done that? Ask for something but take no time preparing to actually receiving it? Live your life's purpose as you dance through your journey, she says, showing others how to find their own rhythm and putting their best foot forward. We all have an inner child that sometimes needs attention. **Tonia Browne** looks to her inner child to free herself of obstacles that were holding her back from multiple victories throughout her life. She shows us how partnering and respecting both spaces, allows the inner child to respect the adult who is now grown up and in charge. **Michelle Reese** loves knowing that everyone has Superpowers! Acknowledge it and Use It! Superpower Self, Engage!!!! **Kimla Dodd** tells us a story I'm sure a lot of us can relate to. The story about "difference" in which YOU are the one who is not "normal." Having Spiritual gifts can make even the most beautiful, loving child an outcast if they are in an unsupportive circle. But, Kimla tells us how this "difference" gave her great joy and the ability to bring wonderful "gifts" to people who needed to hear a *whisper* from beyond. And while Dodd "found" her gift, **Renee Essex Spurrier** writes about losing <u>and</u> finding the gift of Hope, simultaneously, in blessed harmony. A truly touching story. **Linda Lee**

teaches us the valuable lesson that we have heard a thousand times, yet, some of us are still not getting it, that sometimes, the validation that you can truly believe in, comes from within. Maybe you'll finally get it after reading her story. **Deborah Bates** writes with great melody, about the colors of life that brighten our pathways of life's journey and **Brenda Fedorchuk**, through trial and error, then errors and trials, comes back to the same conclusion. She IS ENOUGH! **Katina Gillespie** describes, in the rawest of forms, how we sometimes are so blinded by the trees that we don't realize how our struggles exist to provide light to others who are in need. **Catherine Madeira** tells a story of how she finds herself in the dreams and realities of others for a higher purpose. Her stories of past, present, and yet to happen future are fascinating. The wings of an Angel continue to comfort and guide **Elizabeth Candish**. Have you felt them yourself? After reading her eye-opening experiences, you may feel that you have. What do Rock and Roll, Kittens, and Trust have to do with one another? Read **Janine Forder's** chapter and forever be a fan! **Donna Jutras Tobey** does a wonderful job showing you that by changing your perspective and changing *what you are looking for,* can open up doors of opportunity or a more enriched life. She says it's easy … if you simply look for Life! Or you can approach life and all of its wonderment and challenges beginning with the all encompassing, Love, as suggested by **Brenda Penn**. Another captivating story is the story of **Barbara McKay**, who began her journey of awakening and overcoming with the onset of her own death. A peaceful life she lives from "knowing." At one time in her life, **Hellen Romphf**, liked to play God - like so many of us have done from time to time. It is exhausting, right? Hellen teaches us how to get out of our own way and enjoy life! When you finally move yourself out of the way, opening pathways that lead to gifts and blessings, don't forget to Let Go, Look Within and Listen to your heart says **Angela Serna**. Reading **Chelle Thompson's** piece is direct and to the point. Like most, I'm sure you've had your fair share of drama in your life. Some good things, some, not so good. I bet you didn't think that in spite of it all, you would be chosen to be one of God's helpers ... with a mission to influence the world? Yes, You! Following the *Divine Whisper* will allow you to be at the EXACT right place, at the EXACT right time, with the EXACT right person that you're supposed to connect with. Even if it's in the middle of a winter day filled to the brim with a temperature below freezing. When you think you are late, you are actually right on time - like **Lisa Hardwick** was as described in her inspirational story of fate. Much like experiencing the sensation of fulfillment after a good meal, **Marci Cagen** closes this journey of *Whispers* with a rich meditation that will whisper to the Divine voice that lies within *you*. A wonderful close AND beginning to a spiritually enriching journey that began with the first story.

You may not have met any of these authors but their stories will sound and feel familiar to you. You may actually see your so-called "random experiences" in a totally different light ... a spiritual light that illuminates *your own* spiritual abilities, gifts and talents. I thoroughly enjoyed reading *Whispers of the Heart*. I was emotionally moved, spiritually rejuvenated and inspired by each and every story. Page after page, you will be introduced to the processes of listening to your own *Divine Whispers* that exist in everyone's life. Allow yourself to heal through their stories. Perhaps your soul will be tapped deep enough that you will hear your own *whispers* of the Heart, Mind, Body and Spirit. Be patient, be diligent, focused and positive. If you stand still, stand quietly, and believe that you are capable; you will hear the *Whispers of the Heart* and be Forever Changed.

Enjoy!

Namaste'

Dr. Janice Marie Collins
www.janicemcollinsphd.com

The only real valuable
thing is intuition.

~ ALBERT EINSTEIN

Angela N. Holton

ANGELA N. HOLTON is a Heal Your Life® Coach and Workshop Teacher, Speaker, Writer, and Founder of Love Sanctuary, an inspirational platform committed to sharing positive messages on healing, growth, Love, and purpose.

Angela resides in New York City where she spends time with her family and close friends. She is an enthusiast of world travel and immersing herself in arts and culture. Angela has found her passion in teaching workshops and coaching her clients to loving themselves more deeply and living their optimal life. She is committed to learning, growing, and loving herself more each day!

Visit Angela at lovesanctuary.com

Pathway to Miracles

"Follow your heart!" We hear this adage and homily frequently as young children and young adults. Our parents, grandparents, and teachers, often encouraged us early in life to live our dreams and listen to our hearts. "Do what makes you happy." We often hear.

I believe there is a Divine plan and purpose for our lives that is created and assigned to us at birth. We are each given the blueprint of who we are, where we will go, and whom we will meet along our way. Our Spirit, which whispers guidance to our heart, is always available to help and protect us. It directs us to the right people, the right circumstances, and the right opportunities to grow and evolve our Souls, which leads us to our life's mission and purpose. But, if we do not quiet our minds to hear the sage advice of our inner guide, or we neglect listening to its wisdom, we may find ourselves off course, experiencing pain, disappointment, and hardship. Our inner guide, our higher Self, always desires what is best for us and will only lead us to our highest good. Notwithstanding our occasional transgression from our path, we can always find our way back. Opportunities are always given to us for rejoining our Path. The goodness of Spirit will always wait and welcome us back to our awakened Path and encourage us to walk boldly and unabashedly toward our passion and purpose.

When I was a young girl, I recognized that I was a very sensitive child. My siblings and cousins called me "cry-baby" and often taunted me until big tears welled in my eyes. "Look, she's going to cry," they said jokingly, and each time big tears fell down my face. For years, I was embarrassed and ashamed of my sensitive nature and viewed it as a weakness. But, later in adulthood, I discovered that my sensitivity is indeed a strength. Through my sensitive disposition, a unique ability and gift emerged, one of empathizing, nurturing, and sharing compassion toward others. Since childhood, I have been deeply connected and sensitive to my own emotional needs, which has enabled me to connect to the feelings and needs of others.

Throughout my life, this connection to myself allowed me to unknowingly follow my instincts, my dreams and desires. Before cultivating a deeper spiritual practice, I lacked the awareness that my Spirit was actually guiding me and I was listening to its whispers. Some of my friends believed I lived a so-called "charmed" life. But, what seemed like a "charmed" life to others was really my practice of listening and following the internal stirrings and desires within me, followed by my intention and hard work. Surely there were many times I ignored that internal voice, which invariably led me to pain and disappointment. In fact, my greatest disappointments and pain came when I ignored the voice admonishing me, "stay clear, this is not for you." Yet in the instances that I not only heard the direction from my heart, but also followed its instruction, life opened up and revealed to me the most beautiful and miraculous experiences. When I listen and adhere to Spirit, I am led to the most kind, loving, and inspirational people, and experience incredible synchronicities and "once-in-a-lifetime" moments. As I began to deepen my spiritual practice over the last three years, my ability to hear and listen to the whispers of my heart has strengthened dramatically.

Receiving the "Loudest" Whisper From My Heart

The most profound and impactful message from my heart sounded more like a thunderous roar than a mild whisper. My beloved dog, Kobi, suddenly passed away in January, 2014, leaving my heart shattered into little pieces. He had been my beautiful, constant companion for nearly 14 years. I travelled the world with him and cared and nurtured him with all of my heart. He was my heart! He was the baby, the miracle gift that I yearned for deeply within my heart to love and nurture. So, when he suddenly left his physical form, my heart cracked open and a deep pain and heartache I never knew before, came pouring out. All of my old wounds resurfaced, betraying the belief that they had been healed or neatly tucked away. They reopened with great intensity. Still, in the searing and unbearable moments of my deepest pain and despair, I heard the clearest and loudest message from my heart. As I sat on the edge of my bed, crying inconsolably and in utter disbelief that he was gone, my Spirit clamored,

"Angela, be the Love that Kobi gave and taught you. He came into your life to teach you. Now you must love yourself unconditionally as he loved you and make it your mission and purpose to teach and share his unconditional Love."

The voice from my Spirit reverberated so loudly, as if someone was in the room with me. I sat there dumbfounded and spoke to my Spirit.

"How can I teach Love? I don't know how to teach Love. It is not possible for me to teach Love. It is too big a task for me." I said to Spirit.

"You don't have to know or learn anything. Just BE Love. Show others unconditional Love simply by being Love and loving yourself unconditionally!" Spirit whispered.

It seemed a tall and impossible order, but in that very moment, my life changed in the most powerful and beautiful way, and I have not looked back. It was the first time my Spirit spoke to me with such power and conviction. I could not ignore it.

In the days following Kobi's passing and the powerful conversation with my Spirit, I knew I had to answer the call and step fully into my purpose of Love. I reflected on the few months prior to Kobi's passing, when I experienced deep stirrings and desires to discover and culti-vate my life's purpose. I desired and searched for greater meaning to my life and received subtle signs that I had a greater calling. After spending the last few years reading books from spiritual luminaries, for my own spiritual growth and edification, I developed a quiet urge to become a spiritual teacher myself. After Kobi's passing, this urge became quite clear.

Excited to begin my assignment, I started with clearing out the people and things that were no longer serving me. I committed to sharing my time only with those who love and support me and who raise my vibration. I made the pledge to love myself unconditionally by showing up for myself no matter what, accepting all parts of myself without judgment and consternation, and living more fully by honoring my dreams, desires, and purpose. The greatest gift of Love I could give myself, my Spirit, and Kobi, is to live for my purpose.

Since my declaration, I have committed every day to learning more about myself, healing my heart, and growing in Love. By surrendering to my pain and following my inner guide, I gave birth to my new baby, Love Sanctuary, my spiritual business. It is an inspirational platform that focuses on healing the heart, growing in Love, and living a life with deeper meaning and purpose, through coaching, leading workshops, speaking, and writing. Each day, I have allowed my heart to guide me in my business venture, including selection of the business' name, my writings, teachings, and inspirations. Discovering my new passion and committing to my life's purpose has given me deeper satisfaction, peace, and acceptance of my life. I am more inspired than I have ever been before to study, learn, grow, and heal my own heart, as I inspire others to do the same. This passion allows me to be my most authentic Self and share the best parts of me with the world. Although letting go of Kobi was a painful sacrifice, losing him guided me to my purpose. I transformed my pain into power, peace, and purpose, which became my healing and fueling power to create, persevere, and strive for a successful business, as well as to heal my own heart. I cannot imagine my life today if I had not listened and answered the call of my heart. It saved my life! Perhaps I would still be immobilized by pain and despair, with feelings of hopelessness. I would not have found the work that I absolutely love or deeper meaning to my life. I am forever grateful that I listened to my heart and for the miraculous change it has created in my heart, my life, and my soul!

Listening To The Whispers Of Your Heart

The ability to listen to the whispers of the heart is not unique to me. Having a connection to one's Spirit and inner guide is available to all of us. It is why we are here. We are all created, not only to experience life as Humans, but also to grow and nurture our Souls. We each have access to our internal compass, our higher Selves, which will always guide us in the best direction for our Soul's growth and evolution. Spirit never desires to see us in pain and suffering. Its mission is to guide us to Love and healing. We often hurt ourselves when we do not listen to our gut, that internal voice, telling us that something or someone is not meant or designed for us. As humans, we are free moral agents. So, in spite of having divine wisdom that places whispers on our heart, we have free will to make our own choices. But we choose best for ourselves, when we listen to those whispers and choose from our higher place, our awakened, fully authentic, most fearless, and most loving Self. We can avoid a lot of pain and suffering if we listen to and follow our "gut" feeling! When making tough decisions, it is important for us to go inward and listen to our hearts and align our choices with our highest and best Self.

How To Turn Up The Volume To Your Spirit

In order to crank up the volume to our Spirit, our minds need to be clear and silent enough to hear from it. Our minds are often cluttered with old, negative thoughts and emotions, which feed and grow the

Ego. The Ego mind lives and thrives in perpetual fear, insecurity, and doubt. Fear-based thoughts of the Ego include fear, anger, rage, jealousy, envy, lack, guilt, shame, apathy, judgment, unworthiness, and un-forgiveness. The Ego aims to control us and keep us in anguish and suffering. It does not aspire to teach, heal, grow or nurture our Souls. While our higher Self, that of Spirit and our inner guide moves us in the direction and flow of Love. Love-based thoughts from our higher Self, include those thoughts and actions of Love, compassion, forgiveness, gratitude, abundance, kindness, empathy, and joy. We connect and communicate with our Spirit through Love. Thoughts and feelings of fear and un-forgiveness, two of the heaviest and most dense emotions, often interfere with our ability to connect and hear our Spirit.

One of the first steps we can take in strengthening the channel to our Spirit is in searching our hearts and our minds for old feelings of fear, anger, and un-forgiveness. Who are we unconsciously still angry with? Who do we need to forgive? Do we need to forgive ourselves? What are we afraid of? Forgiveness can be a lifelong process with many layers, but each time we remove a layer, our hearts soften a bit more. Writing a letter of forgiveness to another person or to ourselves, then safely burning it, can help us release old emotions. We can also practice daily visualizations where we imagine forgiving and releasing the other person and ourselves, while repeating, "I forgive you. I accept that things cannot be different and I release myself." Repeating this as often as possible is a very powerful practice. Journaling about our anger is also a healthy and powerful tool. The key is to practice consistently.

Choosing Between Our Head & Our Heart

Everyday our struggle is in choosing between our Ego and our heart, between fear and Love. There are no neutral thoughts or actions, so whether consciously or unconsciously, we always choose a thought. As easy as we choose a negative thought, we can train our minds to think and focus on positive thoughts. Concentrated thoughts of fear and worry are misaligned with Love and can interfere with our connection to our higher Selves. A daily gratitude practice can help train our minds to focus on good, loving thoughts. We can attempt to find the good in all things. Gratitude is the pathway to happiness and when we are happy our energy vibrates at a higher frequency, which heightens our connection to our hearts. A daily exercise of writing 5-10 things that engender feelings of gratitude is a helpful practice in shifting our thoughts.

We can also begin to choose and think more loving and positive thoughts about ourselves by removing the negative beliefs and old programming we have come to believe about ourselves. The direction in which our life flows tells us the unconscious thoughts we are keeping about who we are, what we deserve, and what we are capable of. These old belief systems and blocks, typically learned in childhood, prevent us from hearing and, more importantly, following our intuition. If we believe we are unworthy of goodness, we may ignore the calls of our Spirit that bring us to greatness and the lives we deeply desire. Therefore, our task in adulthood is to unlearn and shift from our old programming. We can shift our beliefs by first recognizing the old stories we are telling ourselves by quiet listening and reflection. Then we can turn those negative statements into powerful affirmations. Affirmations are positive statements that we use to counteract the negative stories we have been telling ourselves. But affirmations only work with consistent use and practice. We can repeat our affirmations frequently in our mind's eye, out loud, in meditation, and in writing.

Learning to decipher from the voice of the Ego from the voice of our Soul and higher Self is paramount to enhancing and understanding our Spirit's call to us. An easy question to ask ourselves when faced with decisions is what would Love do? If our choice leads us to anything besides Love, then we know it is the voice of the Ego. Whispers from our heart will always lead us to feeling Love, joy, and compassion, because

Spirit is pure and unlimited, unconditional Love. Spirit will guide us to abundance, success, and Love. The more we practice listening and understanding the cues from our bodies and other signs, and perhaps faltering from time to time, the more we understand ourselves and the individual and unique expression of our own intuition. Our communication becomes stronger. Like any relationship, we cannot build a strong relationship with our Spirit, without first developing it, then cultivating and nurturing it.

Miracles and Meditation

A self-taught meditation practice I began a few years ago was the magical medicine that fundamentally changed and gifted me with the miracle of mindfulness, present moment awareness, and strengthened my ability to hear my inner guide. By quieting the internal and external chatter of my mind through meditation, and focusing on the present moment, I began to listen, know, and understand my internal guide. The quieter we become, the more we can hear our Spirit. Our lives can be busy and hectic and if we do not slow down enough and quiet the noise, we may miss important guidance and wisdom that our Spirit calls out to us. Stillness allows us to hear the whispers of the heart. But once we hear it, it is up to us, and only us, to follow the call. Our Spirit never forces us.

Developing a meditation practice is one of the greatest gifts we can give ourselves. Meditation helps us gain better control of our thoughts by bringing conscious awareness to the thoughts we keep. As we become more mindful of our thoughts, we learn to release negative and fear-based thoughts and shift our thoughts to positive, higher frequency thoughts. It is through higher thoughts of Love, compassion, forgiveness, gratitude, peace, and joy that we connect with Spirit and our higher Selves. We connect through Love. It is always about Love.

Love is the language of our Divine Source. We cannot connect or create from any other place than Love.

 "Love is the bridge between you and everything."

~ RUMI

Our inner guide is always available to us, waiting for us to call on it. But it is our task to remove the layers of negative emotions that may cover our hearts. As we grow in more loving thoughts and align with higher frequencies and bring our attention to the present moment, we experience greater synchronicities and miracles in our lives. Miracles happen in the present moment. When we hear our intuition on a soul level our lives begin to naturally flow in the direction of Love and miracles. When miracles begin showing up for you, record them in your gratitude or miracle journal. The more you listen to the whispers of your heart and acknowledge the miracles that show up in your life, the more guidance you will receive and the more miracles you will experience.

A Simple Meditation Practice

An ideal meditation practice is 20 minutes, twice per day. Once in the morning and another in the evening. Begin by sitting in a comfortable position, whether in a chair, a bed, or the floor. The key is to be comfortable because if we are not comfortable it is difficult to continue any practice. I like to place my left hand over my heart, which is the closest connection to the heart, and my right hand over my lower abdomen. Begin taking slow deep inhalations and exhalations. As your body begins to relax, check in with your heart. I ask my heart each morning, "How do you feel?" Then I listen and allow whatever comes up to express itself.

Before starting your meditation ask your Spirit to guide you to whatever you need to know. Then begin slow and deep breaths in and out, paying attention to your breath as it moves from your base, the root chakra, to your throat chakra. Notice the rise and fall of your abdomen and chest as your breath rises and falls. Keep your attention on your breath. You can count your breaths; inhale-exhale 1, inhale-exhale 2, etc. or you can repeat a mantra, which literal translation is 'instrument of mind.' A mantra is a tool to aid in concentration during meditation. You can use your affirmation to repeat as a mantra while meditating, such as, "I am beautiful, perfect, whole, and complete." If your mind wanders, allow it to, but gently bring it back to counting your breaths or using your mantra. When the thoughts come, allow them to come and then pass without judgment. Keep gently coming back to your concentration. I like to bring my attention and awareness to the energy and vibration of my heart. I have found that the deeper this connection to my heart, the more I feel its vibration throughout my body. Sometimes, when I feel great joy, it feels like my heart is singing to me. You can also play soft meditation music or listen to guided meditations, both can be found in abundance online and on YouTube. There is a bevy of research and information available to us about different forms of meditation. What is most important is finding a technique that is suitable and comfortable so that we commit to a practice. Whichever we choose, our Spirit is there, waiting to connect. It has infinite knowledge and wisdom to share with us. Our only task is to be still and listen to its whispers to our heart!

Dedicated to my sweet Kobi, my angel and spirit guide — you taught me unconditional Love and compassion. Because of you I have found purpose and meaning to my life. With you forever in my heart, we can pursue our mission together. I am extremely grateful for your guidance and I love and miss you with all of my heart!

My deepest Love and gratitude is given first and foremost to the Divine Source that dwells in me forever. My mom and dad, I love you both. You are my BFF's and I am glad I chose you as my parents. My Nana, Aunt Carol, my beautiful Sisters, my only Brother, Family and dearest Friends, thank you for your love and support. I love you! Granddaddy and Kobi, continue to guide and watch over me. A special thank you to Igal Fedida, you saw this before I did! Thank you Dr. Dee Watts-Jones. To all the spiritual teachers and soulful lessons that have shown up to teach me, heal me, and make me better, my heart overflows with gratitude!

~ Angela N. Holton

Debbie Ledford

DEBBIE LEDFORD is a Heal Your Life ® Coach, Workshop Leader and hypnotherapist. She is dedicated to helping people make life-changing transformations. She is an advocate for families who have children that suffer from mental illness and has been a support group facilitator for many years. She resides in Grass Valley California, where she spends time with the loves of her life, her husband, children and grandchildren.

🌿 Stop, Look and Listen

I t is a cold frosty morning in Beeville, Texas. I am six years old. My mom has come into my room and she is slowly waking me with her soft gentle kisses on my cheek, whispering in my ear, that it is time to get up. It feels so right to have this moment with Mom, in the quiet still morning. I treasure the moment, feeling warm, toasty and safe in my soft bed. I know that I soon must get up and start my day. My mom was a young mom with a big responsibility raising five children while my dad was in the military. We lived in military housing. Lots of the dads in our neighborhood were away and most moms did not drive.

This was the early 1960s. The neighborhood children all walked to school together, the older children looking out for the younger ones. Even as a little girl, a part of me knew that my mom was terrified to send me out in the cold, dark morning to walk to school. The school was not far, but we had to cross a major highway. Each morning my mom cautioned me to be very careful, pay attention and stay with the other children. So I was taught to be very mindful as I walked to school. I felt my mother's fear in the cells of my being. I sensed the seriousness of following her instructions. I knew that once I got to the highway it was of the utmost importance to stop, be alert and cross carefully.

Once we got to the other side of the highway, there was a profound change in my energy. My spirit felt light. The fear was gone and the typical playfulness of a child returned. This was my first experience of noticing how different emotions and energies felt in my body. I could feel there was a connection with what was on my mind and how my body was feeling.

As the end of our school day drew near, I felt the energy shifting again. Our teacher would start getting us ready for our journey home. I could feel the seriousness set in again. We would sing a song, with words preparing us for our journey home. The words went like this **"stop, look and listen if you expect to grow up tall."** We would practice stopping at the highway, looking both ways for cars, and listening for the sound of cars that might be coming, but were not yet within our sight. We were taught not just to use our sight to ensure our safety, but also our hearing. But the thought that stayed with me the most was to stop, be mindful and use my full attention for that big moment when we would be crossing the highway.

This experience has stayed with me my entire life. The words Stop, Look and Listen were imprinted on my cellular memory. My internal wisdom stored these thoughts and feelings away, knowing that they would be of value to me as I traveled the great highway of life. I would like to share with you, how as an adult, I have taken this lesson and used it to connect with my inner wisdom. I have learned the importance of connecting the feelings I have within my body to my emotions, and then stopping to look at the situation and to check in with my heart and hear what it has to tell me. I call this the Stop, Look and Listen Process. But, before I go further with the details of this process, I want to share a little bit about how the heart functions.

The heart is truly amazing. It is a muscular organ that pumps blood to all the tissues in the body through a network of blood vessels. The right side of the heart pumps blood through the lungs where it picks up oxygen. The left side of the heart receives the blood containing oxygen and pumps the blood to the rest of the body. The heart is an organ that is so important, so vital, that if it quits working, our life is over. It is truly necessary for every moment we are alive here on the planet. However, my life experience has taught me that the heart has another function, and that is to house our soul, our inner wisdom and our emotions. Think about it for a moment. When we experience emotional pain, we feel a true ache in our heart. Have you ever experienced that ache in your heart? Maybe it was loneliness, loss or disappointment. On the other hand, have you ever noticed that feeling in your heart when you are full of joy? For me it is a feeling of fullness, completeness, being energized, just knowing that in this moment all is well.

When I feel content, I feel it in my heart. It is almost like a feeling of euphoria throughout my entire being, but it most definitely starts in my heart, my soul space. I believe the heart is a physical body part that is essential for keeping us physically alive. Yet, it is also there to bring wisdom, knowledge and emotion into our lives. I often think, if my heart can keep all the organs in my body going, without me even thinking about it, surely my heart can guide me in my times of need.

The Stop, Look and Listen process gives me the time and silence I need to connect with my heart and truly hear the wisdom it has to share. I have learned not only to rely on just one of my senses, but to check in with all my senses. I know that if I have an uneasy feeling in my body, it is a signal that it is time to Stop. Stopping might look like taking time to be alone, to journal, meditate, pray or listen to music that helps me get in touch with my inner wisdom. The main principle is to just Stop. Don't charge ahead.

Once I have connected with the feelings in my body, I look at the feelings and examine them. I find the words that express what I am feeling. Then I ask myself a series of questions that will help me better understand what message this feeling has for me. Some of the questions might be: What is my belief about this feeling? Is it my own belief or is it a belief that came from someone else? Is it true? Does it serve me? Is it for my highest good?

I believe my life is a manifestation of what is going on in my inner world. This is where I ask myself am I happy with what I see? Do I feel spiritually connected? Do I feel fulfilled? You will have your own questions for which you are seeking answers. Spending time alone with yourself is the only way to develop that skill of looking deep within. It takes courage to look into every part of your soul. Of course there are the parts we admire, but we must also look into every emotion that lives in our heart. We must look into the place where emotions like fear, loneliness or disappointment may live. Once you have the courage to look — then it is time to listen.

In the stillness, I tune into my heart and listen. If I have the courage to hear what my heart has to tell me, and act upon that knowledge, I can do amazing things. Because the knowledge that lives within my heart is what fuels my passion and gives me my real, authentic power. When I tap into my inner wisdom that lives within my heart space, I can do anything. I believe this is true for everyone. In the whispers of our hearts there is divine guidance. The heart can be our compass that will guide us through any storm or lead us triumphantly through an adventure. It is the inspiration that we need when we want to make a difference in the world. When we feel stuck, if we dare to get quiet and still, there will always be a whisper to guide us and encourage us. We need to not only hear what our hearts have to say — but we need to live in complete trust, knowing that the information we seek is always there waiting for us.

I believe that God has given all of us everything we need, right inside of us, to have the most incredible, amazing life we can imagine. But — it is up to us, if we will take the time to stop, look and listen to that amazing well of wisdom and intuition that lives within our heart.

I would like to share with you a meditation I use when working my way through the Stop, Look and Listen Process. The first thing you need to do is find a quiet, comfortable place. For me that is on my back deck. There is a very old cedar tree that grows beside it. The energy of this tree helps me feel very grounded and connected to my authentic self. Only you know what that place will look like for you. Perhaps it is a setting in nature, or a special room or chair in your home. The main things are, it needs to be a spot that is readily available and calls to your spirit. You need to feel nurtured and safe. Once you get settled and comfortable allow yourself to just sit and breathe. Notice what it feels like with each breath that you take. Feel the oxygen coming into your body. Now notice what it feels like when you exhale and you allow the oxygen to leave your body. Notice how your chest rises and falls each time you inhale and each time your exhale. Can you hear your heart beating? Put your hand on your heart and feel it beating. Tell your heart how grateful you are for all it does for you, physically and emotionally. Allow your heart to feel the immense appreciation you feel for it.

Now, tell your heart that you are here, to listen. That you desire to hear all the wisdom it has for you. Be patient. Allow yourself to just be in the stillness; knowing that with each breath comes wisdom, answers, intuition and guidance. Listen with your heart, your soul and your entire being. As the wisdom comes to you, you may want to start to write in your journal. Don't think about what you are writing, just let it flow. As the wisdom flows, continue to allow yourself to be in a state of gratitude. Thanking God, the universe, the angels, your spirit, your higher consciousness and anything else that comes to you. This is the time to ask your inner wisdom about the big questions in your life while trusting that all the information you need comes to you. Allow yourself to absorb every bit of treasured information and sacred wisdom you receive. If you choose not to journal during this process, be sure to journal afterwards. As you write you will be using the sense of touch, this will help anchor the information into your cellular memory, where it becomes a part of you.

Once you feel you are complete with receiving information and expressing gratitude, take a few moments to see yourself breathing love, peace and serenity into your heart; and then as you exhale, see yourself releasing anything and everything that no longer serves you. See the love, peace and serenity coming into your heart and filling every cell of your being. You now see that you are so full of love, peace and serenity that it can no longer be contained within you. So you see yourself traveling the great highway of life, and as you do this you reach out to others and share this love, peace and serenity with them. Now allow yourself to see the impact you can have on the planet by filling yourself up with love. Notice as this love overflows from your spirit, mind and body and then fills the world. When you are ready, come back to the present moment. Remembering and feeling grateful for all the information that you gained during this time of Stop, Look and Listen.

Once you have completed the meditation, give yourself time to absorb all the information and to process it. Remember the whole point of the process is to be in the stillness, so you can hear the whispers of your heart. Taking this time for yourself is a gift to you!

The thought I would like to leave you with is that your heart is full of wisdom to assist you on the great highway of life, the answers are always there — but you may not hear them if you don't take the time to stop, look and listen.

Dedicated to my Mom, Patsy Ann Collier. You always saw me as a writer and believed I was capable of doing great things. You are forever in my heart — I love you.

I would like to express heartfelt gratitude to my husband Mike Ledford and to my children and grandchildren for their love and support. A special thank you to Deanna Leitch and Sue Marshall for being incredible teachers on this journey called life.

~ Debbie Ledford

Tonya Thomas

TONYA THOMAS, M.S. is a Habits & Relationship Coach, family therapist, Reiki Master/Teacher and author. She has a bachelor's degree in business and a master's degree in Marriage & Family Therapy, and will soon complete her doctorate in Psychology.

She resides in central California and enjoys traveling to her home state spending time with her children, grandchildren, family and friends. She also enjoys sharing Reiki through both giving and training others. Her deepest passion is helping people by challenging their limiting beliefs towards finding the love within and empowering them to live their life to the fullest.

Facing the Unknown to Finding the Love Within

March 2011 — I sit here today watching the latest snowfall melting away, although it's late March and should be sunny and warm by now. It's beautiful sitting here watching mother earth being cleansed in preparation for a new journey, a new season promising to bring new life and joy. As I sit here enjoying the beauty, I, too, am being cleansed and prepared for my new journey, a new season promising to bring me new life and much joy. As I prepare to leave a 27-year career in a few months to follow my passion, both excitement and fear are stirring within. However, this is not the first time I've faced the unknown and I'm sure it won't be the last. I remember back to a time when I began a new journey, a time I was forced to embrace my fear of not knowing what lay ahead of me. I was very young at the age of 18 when I left the only life I knew.

It was late into the night as I lay in bed asleep when I was abruptly awakened by the burst of light and an angry voice screaming for me to get up. This voice was calling out horrible names such as, *"You bitch, you slut, you whore…I will kill him!"* The voice then came toward me, grabbing my arm to pull me from the bed and throwing me across the room. I could feel a most crushing fear that totally engulfed me, as I knew right then the man who had controlled my body, my mind, my life had come back to do exactly what he had promised if I ever shut him out. After throwing me across the room, he turned and moved down the hall toward my younger brother's room screaming, *"I'm going to kill* him. *I'm going to take him away from you!*" as he went for a gun. He was going to kill the man I loved, my fiancé. At that moment, it all became a blur and I don't remember running to the living room, but when I got there my mother was screaming "*No!*" and was crying hysterically as she placed her body against the front door. I quickly ran to the kitchen in case I needed to escape when I saw my brother standing in the hallway showing me bullets in his hand, letting me know the gun was not loaded.

At that moment, I saw my chance to negotiate, in whatever way I needed, to bring calmness back to our family. I began talking to my step-father in a calm, soft and loving voice telling him how he could come back into my life and we could then be the family we once were. He started to cry as he let go of the gun and sank down onto the floor. As I stood there watching, I felt a deep sadness as my mother fell to the floor in exhaustion, and yet I could see the relief in her eyes when I told them we could be together as family again. I had seen her eyes so full of pain over the weeks before while he was in jail and listened to her continuous begging of me to forgive the one man she loved for hurting me all those years, so that she could be with him again and no longer feel alone. As I stood there looking at my mother, her sadness reminded me of the first time I saw her in pain, I was only seven years old.

"We were very poor and had no beds to sleep on. Our beds were made of blankets laid out onto the hard wood floor. Food was scarce and my mother ate only after we had finished. Then one afternoon my mother was very sad. I watched as she carefully placed towels under the doors and had us lay down on the bed made of blankets. The sun was still shining and I wondered why we had to go to bed so early. Then I saw her turn on the gas stove and blow out the flames, allowing the fumes of gas to fill the air. I silently watched as my mother prepared for us and herself to die as she could no longer handle her sadness. She then picked up the phone while she cried and reached out for

*help. It was a day that I would forever remember and I knew I would
always have to protect her. Little did I know what that meant until
the day she met a man who soon became my step-father. I remember
looking up at him as he smiled down at me. I did not like him, but
my mother was happy."*

The house that night became very quiet, a tranquility of peace as everyone went to bed, that is everyone but me. When morning came, I left
and never returned.

I am forever grateful to Jeff and his family for taking me in and
giving me a safe place to be. They accepted and loved me without judgment and taught me what a healthy family was about. I began a new
journey that scared the hell out of me, and yet I was free from the life
I once knew. I soon had my own apartment and although I felt a sense
of freedom, I still felt fear. I feared that my step-father would follow
through on all the promises made throughout my childhood years,
promises of hurting anyone who took me away, or if I ran away how
he would find me. This fear was so deeply etched in my body that if a
light was left on at night or there was even a slight sound in the other
room, I would know he was there. It was 20 years later I learned about
triggers of sexual abuse and then realized why I was never able to sleep.
I had to have total darkness and pure silence. Friends would laugh at
me saying, *"That's silly, put a mask over your eyes."* However, it wasn't
actually about seeing with my eyes, but the sense of my body knowing
that he was awake and would be visiting me soon.

It didn't take long before Jeff moved in with me and became my
full-time protector. He would stay with me every night, tucking me into
bed and locking the door behind him as he left to return home. Jeff had
taken on the role of my protector at 17, moving in with me just months
before we married. But I still lived in fear even though he was with me.
Fear that one day those promises would come true and I'd lose the man
so dear to me … and my freedom. I was constantly trying to keep my

balance and deal with my fears, and yet still not feeling like I belonged. I knew my step-father was always watching me no matter what I was doing or where I was. He would come into my work reminding me he was there watching and waiting. Then one day Jeff just happened to be standing behind me and escorted him outside. I never knew what was said, but he never came back.

Over the next few years my step-father continued to reach out to me through my mother. By this time Jeff and I had two children and I had learned to deflect the comments and constant requests to allow him back into my life. I was now strong enough to know that he was incapable of following through on all the promises he made. He no longer had any power over me. I always protected my children by never allowing him to see them and would visit my mother and siblings away from their home. Then one day I received a call from my mother begging me to allow my step-father back into my life. I could hear him in the background coaching her when she said to me, "*I know at such a young age you didn't start the abuse, but you were a part in keeping it going. You benefited from it. You got special privileges the others didn't.*" I remember standing there, Jeff watching as the warmth of my blood drained from my face and body. My only response was, "*Believe what you want. You are no longer my mother.*" and then I hung up the phone.

It was ten years before we spoke again at the hospital when my grandmother was dying. My grandmother, the only true love of my life until my children and grandchildren were born … and I'd now lost her. A few years later my step-father died from a long fight with cancer, and so did my marriage.

I remember the day so well. The day Jeff said he no longer loved me as he cried and turned away. It felt as if someone had just taken their fist, shoved it through my body, grabbed my heart and pulled it from my chest. I couldn't breathe. I couldn't think. All I could do was cry, as I curled up like a baby. I walked around in a daze as if I was a ghost and feeling like everyone could see right through me, as if I wasn't there. I was being launched into a new life, one I did not want. I was facing the unknown, again. My life had been built around my family, so I didn't have many friends. I felt so alone and sad. My heart was so broken. There was nothing but a deep hole left in my body. *WHY...is all I could scream. Why now?* I was just finishing my bachelor's degree. I was growing in my career and now my world just fell apart. As painful as it was, I again embraced the unknown and then I began to grow. It was the right decision for Jeff, as he had been my protector since 17 and no longer needed to fulfill that role. I needed to let him go so that he could find himself apart from my fears and pains that he so carefully and patiently protected. It was time to launch back out into the world so that I could experience life in a new way. And, what a ride it was!

The next five years I call "my crazy life." From 1996 through 1997 I partied as if I were in my 20's, staying out most nights until 3 a.m. and then crawling into bed to get a few hours of sleep before going to work the next morning. I met new people who became good friends and others who quickly passed through. I was a walking zombie with little regret as to who I might hurt, while staying safely out of reach from anyone who might want a serious relationship with me. Coworkers lived vicariously through my adventures of travel and excursions saying, "*You have the life.*" Little did they know how much I cried myself to sleep and kept pushing to keep from feeling. Between 1997 and 2001 I met and married my second husband, helped him fight for full custody of his children, continued to battle the relationship between my children and his, dealing with his and my needs...and not lose me in the process. I had returned to school to get my degree and license as a Marriage and Family Therapist, and then I was divorced in 2001 for the second time. *STOP!!! Let me off this rollercoaster...NOW! I don't want to continue living like this.* So I started asking God, "*Who is this me I'm searching for? Why am I making these choices? Who am I? Why am I here? Please help me!!!!*" Soon after, I met a new friend who handed me a book called, "The Celestine Prophecy." I began reading and it led me to more reading and even more reading. I couldn't get enough. I started paying attention to my surroundings and sitting in silence, really listening this time for answers. I studied things that didn't make sense to me. My brain would hurt, my stomach would ache. I would toss and turn with each new level of learning about why I had experienced what I had.

I always felt a connection to God, but I had never related God to actually being a part of me and how I am connected as ONE with all. I had never thought about something higher or more powerful as this universe and how it all works together in synchronicity. How everything happens for a reason, there are no mistakes. I was blown away when I had a reading one day where the reader asked me what happened at such a young age that dramatically changed my life. It freaked me out how this person could know I had a life-altering change by merely looking at my charted course and his intuitive reading. He told me I chose the parents and the experiences to have before entering this world so that one day I could teach and help others to heal. Okay, now this is way beyond my Baptist upbringing, but why did I feel comfort in this knowledge? Is it possible what he was saying was true?

My world began to change more rapidly now. Doors began to open. I started meeting people who led me to what I needed to learn next and I continued having new experiences that brought me growth; some good and some not so good. If I needed money I'd pray and light a green candle, but always remembering to pray for others too, so as not to be selfish. I'd find money in my mailbox from refunds granted out of the blue, additional work would come my way, and when I was told I had to pay taxes one year I received a call that an entry had been missed and after being corrected, the IRS ended up giving me a refund instead. Now this got my attention in a big way! It woke me up to the flow of the universe…and my life. I was feeling pretty good.

In 2005 I began feeling restless and felt a need to make some major changes in my life. My children had left the home and I was on my own. So…I moved myself to California. Everyone was a bit nervous and yet excited for me, as I was doing this on my own. I was leaving the family and friend cushion and spreading my wings. It was exciting and yet I was really scared … again, jumping right smack in the middle of the unknown. But this time, I was trusting in the decisions I was making and allowing the universe to guide me. The universe has a way of taking us to the right place if we request what we desire, and then we allow it to happen. For example, I had taken on a new assignment at Boeing in Wichita, Kansas to implement an employee improvement program across the enterprise. My first meeting with the group was held in Seattle, Washington, in early February 2005. I had started talking about wanting to make changes in my life and how I would be willing to even move across the country to do so. A month later, I pulled into Southern California just in time to sign my new lease and await the arrival of my furniture.

Then, all of a sudden, as I sat in the middle of an empty room I realized, *"I am alone! Oh my, what did I do? Why did I ask for this?"* It all happened so fast and I began to feel homesick and wanted to return to what I knew. I began to cry myself to sleep again, wishing I could go home. Friends kept asking, *"Why are you not making new friends? Why are you not going out? We believed that if anyone could do this, it would be you!"* It was time to do something about how I was feeling, so I decided to do what had helped me before, and started reading, praying and allowing the universe to guide me. I then began reaching out to a few acquaintances I knew and taking different routes when I went for my walks along the beach. Then one day I made a different turn and happened upon a hair and nail salon, where I made an appointment to get my nails done. During that appointment, the lady who was working on my nails rudely began questioning me about my life and asking me why I was alone. She then introduced me to some beautiful friends who are still dear to me today. My friendship circle grew once more and my life came alive like I had never experienced before. I had a career that allowed me to travel, I lived by the beautiful Pacific Ocean, my children and I grew closer, I had an abundance of friends and I started working on my doctorate. What more could I ask for?

August 25, 2009, my daughter gave birth to my beautiful granddaughter. My heart burst open as I witnessed my only daughter giving birth to her first-born child. On that same day I received another gift, a call totally out of the blue from my high school sweetheart. I had not heard his voice in over 30 years and he just happened to call me on that magical day to apologize for blaming me for breaking his heart. He went on to say that he was a teenager who didn't understand what was really happening and had blamed me for something that was obviously not my fault. He was speaking about the abuse and how he had believed I was protecting my step-father instead of allowing him to help free me of my painful life. He had carried this burden for over 30 years, knowing as a young man there was something seriously wrong. He tried in every way to get someone to listen, even trying to get me to run away with him, but I wouldn't budge.

It wasn't until we shared our sides of the story that we both understood the truth and the impact it had on both of us; and how much it had affected all of our relationships. He never knew until we spoke, how I was only trying to protect him, as I was my mother. I never wanted anyone else to be hurt. The painful memories I carried so deep within my body began to surface. I could actually feel them crawling out of my skin. He kept apologizing, but I kept telling him I needed to hear this and I was at the right time in my life to listen. He became the window of my abusive childhood and a safe place to share, with my knowing he would not judge or think less of me. He shared with me how I had been placed in a position of power over my own mother and siblings, and that I had played the part as my way of surviving. He shared how many of the adults in my life saw something was wrong, but they were either too afraid to speak up or didn't want to know the truth, and so they remained silent. I am grateful to him for coming forward as it was the missing piece I needed to find my "*true healing*" and the release of my childhood scars.

I have experienced both pain and joy in my life by facing many challenges I call *gifts* that have provided me growth and launched me forward to who I am today. I've always been a survivor and never saw myself as a victim. I strongly believe it's up to each of us to find the healing within so that we may live our life to the fullest. I believe we are here to experience love and to help each other live the best life possible ... and be happy! Throughout my life I have always felt guided and protected by something bigger, and once I learned about listening to the "God" that I was one with, I became more aware of when God was speaking to me. I began **asking** for direction, **listening** to my intuition and **allowing** my heart to forgive those who hurt me. I love my life and I love helping others by challenging their limiting beliefs, guiding them to finding the love within, and then empowering them to live the life they desire. I am truly happy and living my life to the fullest each and every day. I'm no longer just a survivor, I am a thriver!

I was once asked, "How does someone go from a 2.0 grade point average to becoming a Doctor of Psychology?"

I believe ... "*Each of us is in truth an idea of the Great, an unlimited idea of Freedom. Everything that limits us, we have to put aside. Don't believe what your eyes are telling you. All they show is limitation. Look with your understanding, find out what you already know, and you'll see the way to fly.*" ~Richard Bach, Johnathon Livingston Seagull

I am flying!

Dedicated to my first love, my maternal grand-mother Jessie Mae Hopkins — because of you, my heart always remains open to love. Dedicated to my children and grandchildren—because of you, the light in my heart continues to shine.

I have much gratitude to my heroes and to all the heroes who provide a loving and safe space for healing and growth. I have so much appreciation for Rick and Margie Lincoln who reached out to help me when I needed it most and who continue to love me unconditionally.

A special thanks to my dear friends, Colleen Williams, Jackie Kranz, Lucy Her and Ricardo Pasalagua—for your incredible friendship and unconditional love. I also want to thank all the teachers and mentors who have crossed my path and provided me with opportunities and support to learn and grow.

~ Tonya Thomas

And no one will listen to us
until we listen to ourselves.

~ MARIANNE WILLIAMSON

Michelle Mullady

MICHELLE MULLADY is a Joyful Living Mentor, International Best-Selling Author, Master Energy Intuitive, Spiritual Guide, and Transformational Healing Workshop Leader who specializes in helping adults and adolescents create healthy and fulfilling lives through spiritual life coaching, energy work, intuitive direction, angelic communication, healing breathwork, simple guided-meditation practices, affirmations, and prayer. Through her individualized, holistic (body-mind-emotions-spirit) approach to life coaching, she can support you to enhance every area of your existence — relationships, health, finances, intimacy, career, and spiritual growth — all while living one day at a time in a busy world.

michellemullady.com

Listen to Your Intuition,
 Your Inner Voice

 "In my heart, I know who I truly am
and what is right for me."

~ MICHELLE MULLADY

There is a universal, unconditionally loving, intelligent life force that exists within and all around you at every given moment. It dwells within you as profound insight, a bright guiding light, and a fluid fountain of inner wisdom. You can open up to this magnificent source and supply of know-how and good judgment through your intuition, a silent super power that tells you what feels correct and accurate for you at that point in time.

Intuition is a natural thing. You are born with that part of your consciousness that acts as a bridge between the physical and non-physical dimensions of your awareness or, as some like to describe it, your inner guru or Higher Self. Simply defined, you have a fraction of yourself that is very capable of viewing the grand plan for your life, and your sixth sense assists you to cross that bridge and enables you to clearly hear your inner wisdom. Following the guidance of the whispers of your heart can put everything in perspective, leading you in the direction of your utmost delight and contentment.

This practical, down-to-earth internal compass allows you to know things, without being aware of how you know them. It is knowledge that seems to come to you from nowhere, a sudden understanding or vision without logical support. Although the basis of this information cannot be figured out by a step-by-step investigation, it is for certain that it's very real divinely-expressed expertise streaming into your conscious awareness — be it the imprecision of a hunch, a gut feeling, vibe or impulse, or a dramatic lightning bolt of brilliance.

Why Developing Your Intuition is Advantageous

 "My intuition is an important resource that can significantly contribute to my happiness and success in all areas of my life."

~ MICHELLE MULLADY

You may be asking yourself why it would be beneficial to commit your time and energy to cultivating the art of listening to your intuition, your inner voice. Quite straightforwardly, because it's one of the most worthwhile things you will ever do for your evolution as a spiritual being having a human experience. In reality it takes fairly little time, and the compensations are colossal.

This is the guidance of the heart. It's a voice that speaks differently from the logical or rational one in your head. How do you tell the difference? The heart murmurs softly; the head chatters loudly.

The head in alliance with the ego has an agenda for your life. It natters away brashly, but its vision is limited and it has its foundation in the realm of earthly illusions. It leaves no opportunities for the mysterious workings of the universe to unfold, nor does it take into consideration the detours your soul has agreed to prior to its arrival on this planet, in order for you to progress on your spiritual path of enlightenment. It's the voice of fear that says, *My way or the highway.*

On the other hand, the inner voice of your heart, sings a different tune. It is an experience of peace, grace, and joy that puts you in alignment with your authentic self. It hums to you in whispers. It softly nudges you in one direction instead of another. It entices you with its tranquility, spontaneity, and the element of surprise. It lives in the power of NOW, never looking backwards into the past or so far into the future that your intuitive hits begin to fog over and cloud your judgment.

Enhancing your intuition empowers you with confidence and clarity so you can communicate clearly with God and the Angels. When your clairvoyant pathway is open, it's easier for you to receive Divine encouragement and counseling. With this information, you can experience more of who you truly are and came here to be. Learning to tap in to your "second sight" removes the fear and confusion that hinders your ability to receive the messages of divine direction that are available to assist you in taking action toward your highest good.

Your finest work, your most excellent moments and your profound bliss happen when you're grounded and centered, listening to and faithfully trusting yourself, allowing your heart and soul to guide you. They happen when you allow yourself to fully, completely, and in love, be led by your intuition.

Believing Intuition

 "When I have faith in my intuition, I am allowing Love to show me the way."

~ MICHELLE MULLADY

If you are like the majority of people in cultures from around the globe, you were taught from an early age NOT to rely on your feelings, not to express yourself candidly and genuinely, not to recognize that you are a unique expression of a loving, mighty, and creative nature. You were probably trained to repress your bursting potential by doing what was expected of you which often includes adopting a strict system of keeping your life's most bona fide truths bottled up inside. Or perhaps you were the one that rebelled against authority, leaving you out of touch with your harmonious self in an equally extreme way. No matter how it took place, I imagine that it was very seldom that you received praise and applause for trusting yourself, validating your own inner accuracy, or owning your power in a truthful and sincere manner. This only leads to feeling like a victim — empty, needy for others approval, and unaided to help yourself. It often results in feelings of rage, desperation, depression, a numbing deadness and separation from your connection to Divine Love. Now that is NOT a life worth living!

The good news is there is a solution and that is to re-educate yourself to take note of and count on the intimate truths that come to you through your intuitive feelings. You must give yourself permission to start acknowledging these extra-sensory "hits". Then, learn to act on them, despite your fears, because the time for playing it safe is just about to disappear. Are you ready? Of course you are! To live in this fashion is frightening at first, as you release the chains that have bound you to a false sense of security created by outdated belief systems, but you will reap the benefits of integrity, wholeness, self-discovery that leads to empowerment, creativity, and the real refuge of reigniting your knowing that you're continually bonded to the energetic current of the universe.

How to Enhance Your Connection with Your Intuition

 "I am patient and gentle with myself
as I learn to listen to the soothing and
trustworthy words of my inner voice."

~ MICHELLE MULLADY

Becoming acquainted with your sixth sense links you to the soul level of your being, making it possible for you to receive wisdom from your Higher Self, the part of you that is directly in touch with the qualities of God and less susceptible to human error. This allows you to co-create your destiny with the cosmos. You will also find yourself in a meaningful relationship with your spiritual identity, opening up your imaginative channels to the sensation of being "in the flow" — a state of synchronization, serenity, love, and pleasure.

Developing your sixth sense begins by listening carefully to what's going on inside of your head, as well as paying attention to the uncommon sensations you experience in your body. This will help you become mindful of your personal interior conversation and decipher the vibrations that are a part of your intuitive system. You can then rewrite the tapes and interpret the feelings as they are taking place, or shortly thereafter. As you become more familiar with your distinctive process, you will begin to notice instinctive occurrences as they arise, and you will then be able to confront them more consciously.

Most people that I work with in my personal sessions and groups find that with a little practice and time, they become steadfastly reconnected to their intuition. Then, they must learn to interpret and act on it in a practical way.

The following five tools will help to awaken your silent super power:

✑ 1. Take It Easy — and Catch Your Breath

Today, learning to relax is vital for developing your intuitive gift, because the pressure of 21st century living can keep you from hearing, feeling, and understanding the messages being sent from the voice of your heart and soul. Monitoring your breathing is one of the easiest and most effective ways to achieve a deep sense of relaxation. When you are under stress, it is common to start to take faster shallow breaths. To relax, you need to reverse the cycle:

Turn on some calming music. Lie on the floor and make yourself completely at ease. Breathe from your diaphragm. Take several full breaths and tense all of your muscles. As you breathe out, fully release the tension and send warm, healing thoughts and energy to every part of your body, starting with your feet and moving up to the top of your head. Try breathing in this style for ten slow inhalations, pausing before slowly exhaling. At the end of this time, you should feel very restful, if not euphoric.

✑ 2. Mantra Meditation

Spiritual practice is essential to reclaiming and working with your sixth sense. Meditating gives you an opportunity to clear your mental airways so that messages of intuition can be heard. Meditation will help you release the prattle of thoughts, ideas, worries, concerns, and things on your need to-do list that muddle your receptive awareness. When you regularly sit peacefully and do nothing, you can achieve the inner stillness that is a prerequisite to letting your instinct guide you to fulfillment and flow.

To meditate, find a quiet comfortable place where you can sit in a relaxed manner, with your spine erect, for five to fifteen minutes a day. Let your thoughts quiet and concentrate on a mantra. As thoughts come into your mind, gently but firmly allow yourself to let them go and return your concentration to your chosen mantra. You can meditate in a comfortable chair, by a lake or stream, in a forest, out in your yard, or anyplace you choose that supports you to unwind and go within.

Here are a few examples of modern mantras:

1. *"Love is the only miracle there is." ~ Osho*
2. *"Be the change you wish to see in the world." ~ Gandhi*
3. *"Every day in every way, I'm getting better and better."*
   ~ Laura Silva
4. *"I change my thoughts, I change my world."*
   ~ Norman Vincent Peale

↭ 3. Grounding

Getting grounded is a process that helps the body to unite with the life-sustaining energies of Mother Earth. Because you are, first and foremost, a spiritual being the physical body sometimes is overlooked or gets neglected, throwing you off-balance. When you are not grounded, you live in your headspace, disconnected from your body, feelings, and the world. It is important to respect and care for the vessel that houses your spirit during your brief incarnate lifetime. This is accomplished simply being aware: of your body, of the present moment, of your breathing, and being linked to the earth.

Being grounded in the NOW (physically, emotionally and energetically) is essential to intuitive living and staying in harmony with your higher vibrations. The benefits of feeling your "foundation" are enormous. When you are grounded you feel composed and centered. You perform in a positive mode throughout the day, and maintain an overall state of wellbeing. You have the potential for awe, gladness, amusement and enjoyment. You have the capacity to experience life with amazement and rapture.

Grounding can be different for everyone, so here are some examples of how you might assist your grounding efforts:

↭ Try a few yoga stretches and poses to refresh yourself.

- ↝ Go to a nearby park or natural setting that you love for the afternoon.
- ↝ Ride your bicycle around the block several times.
- ↝ Invite a dear friend over to chat and share a cup of herbal tea on the patio.
- ↝ Eat a healthy meal outside under the stars.
- ↝ Lay out in the garden on a fluffy blanket with a soft pillow.

↝ 4. Opening the Third-Eye

The major chakra, known most commonly as the *Third Eye,* is located in the center of the forehead and between your two eyes. When it comes to your intuition and your psychic abilities — natural talents that are innate to us all — there is nothing more healing than a vibrant, in-tune third-eye chakra. Having a healthy third-eye chakra can assist you in using your intuition and insight without anxiety and false impressions. When you bring your third-eye chakra into balanced activity, your clairvoyance is unlocked, and you can begin to correctly see what is going on within your life.

Allow yourself to get seated in a position that feels good for you, and meditate for at least five minutes. Now draw your attention toward your *Third Eye* as you visualize a glowing golden-white light surrounding you. Breathe in this golden-white light, letting it completely fill up the inside of your head with its luminous energy. Exhale, and see the golden-white light being released outward into the room through your open *Third Eye.* Repeat this visualization exercise until you see your *Third Eye* blissfully open, radiating the color indigo blue, with sparkles of white and purple lights.

↝ 5. Give Thanks

A favorable everyday practice is to say "thank you" for the many ways in which intuition benefits your life. Gratefulness forms a loving bond between you and your extra-sensory gift, establishing a solid and more active awareness of this vital relationship. You can express thanks for the growing communication with your innate self, by placing one hand over your heart center and saying "I have been blessed" when you receive a perceptive "hit". Gratitude is a superb ambiance of the soul in which your intuition will flourish.

My contribution to this book is dedicated to Divine Love, the true Source of my beautiful life. I dedicate this work to You in sincere gratitude for your unconditional loving light upon us all. Thank you for your faith in me. May your work through me be a blessing in the world.

A special thank you to Chelle Thompson, my writing mentor and editing genius for the past seven years. I truly know that I am the best-selling spiritual author that God intended me to be because of your unwavering love, guidance and support. You have blessed my life beyond measure and helped me to manifest some of my biggest dreams. Our relationship was divinely assigned and organized by the heavens my dear friend. I love you.

~ Michelle Mullady

Trust yourself. You know more
than you think you do.

~ BENJAMIN SPOCK

Gilly Kennedy

GILLY KENNEDY is the creator of Game for Living™ a unique motivational program that inspires people to live a life they love through the medium of "game-play." Using the latest teachings on happiness and success, she offers reality-changing strategies in a fun, enlightening way through online courses, games workshops, coaching, speaking and writing.

Gilly has transformed her own life over the last 10 years and successfully steered her path from an exhausting struggle in the rat race, living a journey of "shoulds," to a deeply fulfilling existence and true happiness. She lives in Edinburgh, Scotland with her partner Tom.

www.gameforliving.com

The Open Window

I wonder if this could be the day. I wonder if there will be a moment today when the light will dawn. I wonder if she is listening, really listening, so that she can hear what I have been waiting to say. I wonder if she is ready.

We are attending a weekend event in London led by one of our favourite life teachers. It is proving to be gorgeously enlightening — the perfect place for receiving words of wisdom and whispering insights. On the first day Gilly asked me a very interesting question, one that seemed to be straight from her heart and one that seemed to get straight to the heart of her existence. Here is what she said.

"I would like to find out how to synchronise my soul with my personality."

Yes I know, it may sound like a huge philosophical question, but I knew exactly what she meant. You see, I am Gilly's soul. Yes, I am her inner being, her true self, her authenticity. I am her shining light. I am her everything, her very essence. I am her vibrant, effervescent energy that flows and sparkles through her body bringing her to life. I am her biggest fan and I love her dearly. Are you getting the picture? Gilly is my personality, my identity and my image to the world. It is through Gilly's personality that I see the world and the world sees me.

Gilly's life has been packed full of experiences, some that felt good, and some not so good. I know them all because I've been with her throughout. It has never been dull. A bit like a roller coaster at various points, as she navigated her way from childhood, through school, university and into the workplace as a manager of change in several large corporations. She has brought two beautiful daughters into the world, nurturing them and guiding them to young adulthood. She has worked hard, overcome many challenges and called on me regularly to give her inner strength to deal with traumas that came her way. We've had many flashes of inspiration together when we have been in sync, totally in tune with each other. She likes to call these *light-bulb moments*! I love that phrase. It so accurately describes what happens when Gilly and I connect with each other. Like she has plugged herself into me and the light has flicked on. I can tell Gilly loves the feeling too, it gives her such a buzz, a warm glow, a radiance that emanates outwards for all to see.

Of course, sometimes her personality decides to switch off the light, and then I have to stay inside — quiet and in solitude for a while. This is when her personality gets a bit carried away with herself and she starts to get out of sync with me. It's when she decides to take on too much and makes herself exhausted. It's when she gives out more than she receives, sacrificing her wellbeing for others. It's when she worries she is not good enough and undeserving of health and happiness. It's when that dreaded unreal fear thing kicks in, threatening to steer her totally off balance. However, Gilly is smart and has come to realise that I am never gone, just hidden behind her personality for a bit.

This is the reason for her question. Gilly wants to find out how we can get better synchronised and not just for those flashing light-bulb moments. She wants to find out how to stay connected before and after the light-bulb moments. She wants to find out how to present me — her exquisite soul — as a person on our planet. And she wants to learn how to see our earth and everyone in it through my eyes — eyes of love, rather than eyes of fear. It's a great enquiry and one that can only be answered when she is ready.

Gilly's been on the alert since she asked her question on the first day and has had her antenna out in all directions listening for answers.

The wonderful news is that yesterday she heard one of my soulmates at the workshop explain something she had never heard before.

"The job of the persona is to be a window to the soul."

Not a lens that is prone to distortion and filtering, but a clear window through which the world can see the soul and the soul can see the world with nothing whatsoever in the way. It was an immense and philosophical question that Gilly had asked and now here was the start of a profound, philosophical answer. Gilly heard it loud and clear.

So with that thought still percolating, we are here on the last morning of this inspiring gathering and I have a strong, knowing feeling that today is the day when I can give her my message.

Let's see how today unfolds...

As we walk into the room where today's discussions are taking place, Gilly asks me *"where will we sit this morning?"* I suggest that she take a seat on the other side of the room from yesterday for a different perspective. She agrees and moves down to the right where she selects a chair opposite two large windows. I'm so glad about that, this is exactly where I want her to sit. *"Thank you for listening, Gilly,"* I whisper. As we wait for the morning session to begin, we are both filled with excitement and anticipation of what lies ahead. Gilly can't wait to receive more details on the answer to her enquiry and as for me — I can't wait to whisper my message to her. Wow! It's going to be a fantastic day.

The leader introduces the next exercise and asks everyone to work in pairs. Each person has to speak for a few minutes with their partner about the ways in which they prevent themselves from being open to receive love. Now that's quite a topic! When it's Gilly's turn to speak, I am so delighted! She says nothing for a minute and appears to be listening intently before speaking. Okay, cool. I get it. She wants me to speak about this from the soul's perspective. She is asking me to give her my message. I can tell that she is ready to get to the heart of it. This is my time! I start things off slowly by whispering a few thoughts to her. Then as she notices the windows on the other wall, I gently say to her.

"You know, Gilly sometimes you don't open the window and let love in. There is so much love out there for you, but if you are to be able to receive it and enjoy it, then first you must open the window. When the window is closed, there is no opportunity for love to flow into your life. No opportunity for the soul to offer its unique, pure love to the world. No opportunity for the soul to be seen in all its glory. Remember that I am your soul. I am the essence of you. I am everything your heart desires. For you to embrace love to the fullest in your reality, then you must be willing to open the window to your soul."

There I've said it! Gilly is listening intently and what ensues is a truly fascinating conversation between the two of us.

She replies.

"Yes, I understand what you're saying. To experience a life full of love then I must allow it into my being and to do that I must first open my soul window! That's a very cool way of thinking about it. I love that and I would love to open that window!"

Great, I think to myself, I knew she was a smart one and that she would get what I mean. Incredible stuff! She continues as one thought after another tumbles out.

"It would feel like a gush of pure love energy flowing through my body. As it bursts in then everything that is blocking the flow will be flushed away, clearing a path for pure love to reach every part of my being. Oh, and if the window is fully open and it's windy outside, it won't just trickle in, it's going to come flying in with full force through that window."

I sense that Gilly is suddenly a little anxious. As her soul, I know these things! I immediately realise that she is worried about something.

"Oh my goodness," she blurts out with more than a dash of concern in her voice, *"What if it's so windy that it knocks me off balance, I might fall over."*

She is suddenly quiet and I sense her listening eagerly for me to speak. Again I whisper, but slightly louder, determined to reassure her. I excitedly remind her of a question that had come up earlier in the day.

"What do butterflies do when it's windy?"

It is a most-glorious question isn't it? I knew Gilly had been fascinated by it.

I see her start visualising the open window and beginning to feel the love energy flying in like a gust of wind. Gilly is seeing herself as a dazzling, colourful butterfly on the inside of the window and as the wind blows into the room, all at once the anxiety is gone and she smiles. I smile too and give her a warm reassuring soul hug.

"Yes you are safe and you can fly. Go on, spread those gorgeous wings of yours and fly. That is what butterflies do in the wind. They flutter their wings and dance without a care in the world. They flit and fly creating graceful patterns as they allow the wind to guide them wherever their heart desires. It's what they are born to do and they love every minute."

Gilly is now immersed in this picture as she encounters an extremely powerful and true discovery.

"I could just go with the flow of love," she says with a tremendous smile from ear to ear. *"I won't fall over or lose my balance. All I do is just open my wings and fly!"*

"Yes exactly," I whisper back, scarcely able to contain my elation. We are both equally excited. *"When you open the window and welcome love in,"* I tell her, *"you make me the happiest soul in the universe!"*

We sit quietly for several seconds, simultaneously gazing out at the window across from us. It is wide open. The sun is shining through, pouring love straight into Gilly's heart and into my soul. People are coming and going, but neither Gilly nor I are aware of them as we savour this spectacular instant. My soul window is fully open. I am Gilly and Gilly is me. We are in perfect synchronicity with each other. We are one.

In the days and weeks that followed this delightful discovery, there has been a much deeper connection between Gilly's persona and me — her soul. We've always been close, but now we're even closer, and not only that, Gilly knows how and when to take a break together and re-synchronise. All she has to do is to bring our special story into her mind and visualise what it feels like to open that window and watch the butterfly spread its delicate, iridescent wings and fly. With that image clear, as if by magic, we become totally in sync again, and when we're in sync, I hear Gilly and Gilly hears me. I see Gilly and Gilly sees me. I am Gilly and Gilly is me. It works every time.

Before I bring this chapter to a close, I thought it would be a lovely idea for me to give you a small gift — from me to you — soulmate to soulmate. That's who you are, you know — my soulmate. As you have been reading this chapter, I have been whispering messages from my soul to yours. Such a splendid thing it is when two souls meet in this way.

So wherever you are, whatever your circumstances, whatever your experience of life to date, I have a special little message to whisper to you.

"Close your eyes and imagine yourself in a room with a window. Then go to the window, open it and as you do so, breathe in deeply and slowly release. There it is done."

"You have just welcomed in an extra bit of love from my soul to yours."

"All is well in your world."

Dedicated to my two very special daughters — Janey and Lucy — who remind me every day of the magnificent gift of love and life.

A huge, heartfelt thank you to everyone I have met thus far in my life, each one of you making me a little bit wiser than I was before.

A special thank you to my favourite life teachers, Louise L. Hay, Dr. Patricia Crane, Dr. Robert Holden and all my fellow Heal Your Life® friends and workshop colleagues for your magic, inspiration and guidance. A final word of thanks to my partner Tom for deciding it was worth a try, opening his heart and loving me just the way I am.

~ Gilly Kennedy

Halina Kurowska

HALINA KUROWSKA is a licenced Heal Your Life ® teacher and Life Coach. She has a BA (Hons.) in Philosophy from the University of Toronto.

Halina is passionate about helping people get in touch with their inner wisdom, empowering them with love and leading them to joy through her workshops and coaching sessions at Living With Awe: Awareness, Wisdom, Empowerment.

She enjoys spending time with her family, her sweet kitty Charlotte, and visiting her son in San Francisco. She loves nature, hiking, practising meditation, reading, writing, lifelong learning, decorating, gardening, travelling and having fun with friends.

halina@livingwithawe.com
www.livingwithawe.com
FaceBook: Living With Awe: Awareness, Wisdom, Empowerment

Spirit Animal

 "Owning our story and loving ourselves
through that process is the bravest
thing that we'll ever do."

~ BRENÉ BROWN

It was just after dawn on a still and quiet summer morning when I veered off the main road at the very last second. I had been following my usual morning route, when a gentle but very persistent voice in my heart guided me to take this detour. That's when I encountered the fox. I was utterly delighted to see such a beautiful animal standing right there on the bridge. I knew, without any doubt in my heart, that the fox had been waiting for me to come driving by. It had willed me to come and see him. I stopped my car in the middle of the empty road and lowered my window. The fox was lovely and not afraid of me at all. I sensed in that moment that there was a deeper meaning and message to this encounter. I had taken the slow road home and had seen something majestic.

"So you're the one who called me to come and see you this morning," I said to the animal. We looked at each other and I spoke a few more words of love and appreciation to this precious creature, so happy about our communion. I believe that we are all connected and that the Universe speaks to us in many ways. Our job is to open ourselves up to the messages and the guidance we receive. We need to be aware and listen.

There was a time in my life when this subtle message from the Universe would have gone unnoticed by me. That was the time when darkness had overtaken my life and drowned out all the light. I am convinced now, as I was then, that this quiet creature was acknowledging the long journey I had taken to regain my worth in the world and showing me I was on the right path.

I had spent the better part of my late twenties drowning my feelings of emptiness and self-doubt in alcohol. Very quickly my occasional drink turned into weekends of bingeing and I would pass out. I found myself, at the age of 30, as a divorced mother of two young children. Even though I found my way to AA and found sobriety shortly after my divorce, my self-esteem was critically low and the sarcastic voice in my head was relentlessly belittling me: "Look at yourself. Look at what you've done with your life. Aren't you just so accomplished and so impressive?"

I was filled with pain and guilt, fear and hopelessness. I felt like I had nothing to cling to in the darkness. My perception of myself, of my life and of the world around me was more than gloomy — it was totally black. Thoughts like "life is full of suffering and pain and sorrow" and even "what's the use" were my constant companion. Up to this point, I had an outlet, an escape into emptiness of not being and not feeling through drinking. Now that this was gone, how was I going to cope?

In the deep darkness that surrounded me, I found a sliver of hope. It came in the form of a tiny voice — a mere whisper really — from inside my heart. "There is another way," this voice said. "Keep searching."

As I have a great love of books and was, at that time, just developing my English language skills, I often found myself at my local library. To help me understand how I had fallen so quickly into alcoholism, I read books on addictions and recovery. This need to understand myself eventually led me to the self-help section. There, a bright and cheerful book with the hopeful title *You Can Heal Your Life* by Louise L. Hay caught my eye.

I thought to myself: "Wow, what a title!!! I can heal my life!!!" And it needed so much healing. Every part of my life was aching in deep pain.

"May this offering help you find the place within where you know your self-worth, the part of you that is pure love and self-acceptance," says the dedication. Later in the book, the author states: "self love and self-acceptance are absolute prerequisites for healing every aspect of our lives."

So I put repairing my extremely shaky self-esteem on the top of my priority list. It was absolutely crucial for me to follow Louise's suggestions and to nurture myself back to wholeness, to heal the huge open wound inside me that was hurting constantly.

"There is so much love in your heart that you could heal the entire planet. But just for now let us use this love to heal you," she writes. With tears rolling down my face I looked in the mirror, as Louise told me to do, and said, "I love you." It was painful. There was so much guilt, shame and self-condemnation. But Louise said, "forgive yourself" and so the process began.

With the determination of a child whose gaze is firmly fixed on the colourful candy in the store window, I repeated the words 'I love and approve of myself' countless times every day.

As we start the process of self-transformation and improvement, others will resent our progress as this shines a light on their own 'stuff'. I found many tried to stop me by saying things like, "You are fine, you don't need to do anything" or "We all are just getting by as we are, we are not 'improving' ourselves so why do you bother with that stuff? Who do you think you are? Do you want to be better than us?"

Their voices echoed the voice of my ego. Most people view the ego as that part of us that is overconfident and boastful, not recognizing that all negativity is actually the product of our ego. Even that overconfidence is an expression of the fear that underlies it. My self-doubt was the expression of my ego, which did not like any improvement and did not like that I was starting to feel better about myself. Ego takes great pleasure in undermining our worth and making us feel very small and unloved and not worthy of a better life. It really likes to keep us down.

Thankfully, the books that guided me on my path and helped me to quiet my ego were presenting themselves rapidly to me. These gems were the balm my heart needed so much. The Spirit whispered through the words on the pages of these books that I was led to pick up.

I knew the only way I could move forward in my life was to adopt the principles set in these books fully, without reservation, with all my heart and practice, practice, practice. Implementing these spiritual principles in my *daily* life was essential. I wanted to be free from all the heaviness in my heart and from all the negativity that was destroying my life.

During the hardest days, the words of Og Mandino came back to me: "Why did you listen to those who demeaned you … and far worse, why did you believe them?"

WOW, that's a statement worth a thousand tears.

My heart knew that I needed healing. Try this, my inner voice said, follow what these books say, this looks like the way out. As I committed to this new path, the changes started taking place: I felt lighter, like the weight of the world was lifted off my shoulders, there was a spring in my step and I started to smile. "Nothing has changed … except you, but you are everything," Og wrote. These words became my motto, the shining light that guided me on my journey into my new life.

About four years after I had stopped drinking and started my self-transformation, I had a conversation with a good friend about education.

"You read that," she asked with slight disbelief, pointing at a thick and scholarly book I was holding and had recently read. "So how come you don't have a degree?"

"Because," I answered. "When I announced to my family that I was planning to go study at the university, my stepmother said, "Have you lost your mind? Who is going to pay for you?"

The friend then said, rather simply, "Well, you should go and get one now."

Immediately my ego balked at the idea. How could I possibly study at a university when I barely speak English? Thankfully, my heart knew what I really wanted. It was a much quieter voice beneath that loud negative shouting in my head but it didn't give up. My heart whispered, "you should give it a try." Although afraid of rejection, I nevertheless started the process of applying. When the wonderful news that I was accepted into the University of Toronto came, I was overjoyed.

I shared this great news of being accepted with the folks in my recovery group as we gathered in a coffee shop after our meeting. I said: "I'm going back to school".

One of them, a middle aged man, asked: "So, are you going to take English classes?"

"No," I answered, rather sheepishly. "I'm going to study at the university."

He almost choked on his coffee. It went splattering all over the table. "University?" he asked after he gained back some composure.

"Yes, the University of Toronto".

I could sense his thoughts: "but she is just an immigrant; yes, she speaks English, but she has an accent and her speech is not that fluent, English is her second language and she is going to study at the University?"

The thoughts I was sensing from him were also my own thoughts of doubt. The voice of my ego was shouting again that I was being silly, that I'd lost my mind thinking I could study at the university and that I shouldn't go. Deciding to ignore the shouting and follow instead the whisper of my heart, I went. And graduated.

Once, in my early recovery, I was asked to tally all my fears. The list was very long. Everyone and everything was there, starting from people and animals through to fears of heights and driving, and many other fears woven in between. It has been a long journey to get from that dark place of self-doubt to where I am today. It started with listening to that small inner voice that whispered to me through the darkness. A whisper that was thankfully able to drown out the loud negativity of my ego and helped me find a road to freedom.

On that fateful morning when I had my encounter with the fox, I had just driven my ex-husband to his job. That in itself was an amazing feat — not only had I conquered my fear of driving, I had also been able to achieve a state of peaceful coexistence with all fellow travellers on this journey called life, which included my ex-husband. I own this amazing transformation to discovering Louise's book and applying everything she suggested. So after restoring my self-esteem to the level that felt good inside, the only natural progression was to reach out to others and to forgive. I repeated many times a day: 'I live in harmony and balance with everyone I know'. That included my ex-husband, my ex-boyfriend, and many others with whom I had had unhealthy relationships.

This practice produced a huge shift in my life and in all my relationships, past and present. I came to the conclusion that I have 'worked out my karma' with my exes — all of them. I've done Louise's forgiveness work, sending them love and forgiving everyone for everything. This does not mean I needed to do this in person. I released them internally in my heart. Life is internal first; our outside circumstances reveal our inner thoughts about life, relationships, and ourselves. Life is inside work.

On my journey I had attempted meditation on several occasions but could not reach the point where I could comfortably say that I meditate. It was all just that: attempts. I wasn't sure how to do it. Should I sit this way or that way? Should I chant some mantra or not? Concentrate on an object? But which object? What about my thoughts? I just didn't have a clue how to go about this.

One day I shared my interest and lack of progress with a friend at work. And, how it usually goes, she shared it with another friend. But, these are good people with compassion for their fellow traveller, so a few days later I received a very succinct email from that other friend. It read: "Vipassana is good and so is The Way of Life". That was all what she wrote in that email. I looked at it puzzled slightly, thinking, "what is she talking about?" Being busy with work and life, I left it sitting in that Inbox for about six months.

Then, one day a thought popped in my mind: "Check the email you got about meditating". This was that special, whispering kind of thought. These thoughts are very gentle and they have a very special quality about them. They feel warm and loving and deep. So I googled "Vipassana". To my amazement I found out that there is a mediation centre about an hour's drive north of my home that offers ten-day meditation retreats. I knew immediately I had to go. This was the kind of call that Mark Twain called "the call of the wild". From time to time I hear its gentle yet persistent command and I feel that I absolutely have to follow it. When I do, amazing things always occur. This is not to say that it's easy to follow it as usually there is an initial fear — at times even a lot of fear — as it was in this case when I decided to sign up for ten days of an unknown experience.

Just reading the course descriptions and rules to observe — student will have to stay for the entire period of the course; noble silence must be observed the entire time; do not pay attention to disturbances of others — left me wondering what exactly I was about to embark on.

"What does it even mean," I asked myself. Does this mean if someone will run amok I should ignore it? What if it will be me? Fearful thoughts started to accumulate. I heard that when we really meditate 'stuff comes up.' What if my stuff came up? Could I handle it? Yet, despite all of these fears, my deep desire to go prevailed.

My son, now a grown man, drove me there. It was a beautiful and tranquil place in the woods. It felt peaceful and serene. A young woman, who was simultaneously very calm and happy, handed me a registration form and a waiver. The waiver stated, more or less, that if I go crazy or die, the Centre is not responsible. Well, that wasn't reassuring. My son and I exchanged looks of fear but I knew this was something I needed to do, to have the experience of silence, of meditation. And the little tiny voice was saying, "You will be okay."

To go through the ten days of silent meditation and reflection is not easy, but it is a richly rewarding experience. Meditation accelerates freedom from attachment and worry, and lessens our ego. There is a statement attributed to Buddha that reflects the truth about the benefits of meditation. When someone asked Buddha what he gained from meditation, his answer was "nothing." But then he added, "let me tell you what I lost: fear, anger, anxiety, depression and insecurity." I know, through my own experience, that this is absolutely true. I'm not a Buddha, but I've lost these hindering qualities as well. I have never felt as free, happy, brave and trusting.

It has been nearly 25 years since those dark days when alcohol controlled my life. The ensuing decades of sobriety have brought me clarity about myself and I've been constantly evolving, learning and embracing the joys of life. Meditating led to an enormous freedom. My view of life evolved. My consciousness evolved. I am at peace with things as they are. And I am so grateful. Following the heart is an awesome thing to do. Since I've started meditating, my life started to really unfold in beautiful ways, the fulfilment of my wishes started taking place. So many wonderful things happened. What's so good now? I am free and happy and joyous and at peace with life. I love my life!

Very shortly after I finished my meditation retreat at the Centre came the day I drove my ex-husband to work and encountered the little red fox. I was listening to Louise's voice on a CD that morning. She was saying, "I am open and receptive to all good." I repeated, "I am open and receptive to all good." I so enjoy her soothing voice and assuring statements. Her wisdom had brought me to that point in my life where I was able to be relaxed and to enjoy the early morning drive. It had also helped me to be open to messages from the Universe. When a small voice inside me said to take a detour through a prettier part of town, I listened and found myself eye to eye with a magnificent fox.

I believe that the Universe communicates with us through many different media at all times, sending us messages that guide us on our path through life. I consulted the book *Animal Speak* by Ted Andrews to see if it would shed any light on the meaning of my encounter. From this book I learned the fox is associated with the art of camouflage and remaining unseen — much like my life had been up to that point. But the book mentions another facet to fox. The animal also represents feminine creative force and is associated with the Tarot card 21, The World. This card "reflects a new world opening up" and that "the process of creation is beginning. It reflects that the world is growing and shape-shifting itself into new patterns that will be beneficial." I like that.

This little red fox on the bridge is my spirit animal — a representation of my life. Hidden for so long under the burden of self-doubt and fear, I am now free to love myself and to share that love with others. I am free to bask in a joyful lightness of life.

I lovingly dedicate this chapter to my sons, Wit and Mateusz, whose amazing Souls chose to share this lifetime with me. Blessed be both of you.

And to all who are still struggling, unsure about their path. I hope my words will uplift and inspire you to always follow the whispers of your heart.

I thank the Universe for guiding me step-by-step on the journey of my life. I am thankful for every lesson and every teacher I met along my way. For it all was a blessing and I am blessed by it all.

I thank my lovely editor Izabela Jaroszynski for fine-tuning my story.

Very special thanks to Lisa Hardwick for having a big trusting heart that brought about the fulfilment of my dream. I am forever grateful.

~ Halina Kurowska

Systems die; instincts remain.

~ OLIVER WENDELL HOLMES

Michéle Hatfield Quesenberry

MICHÉLE HATFIELD QUESENBERRY is a teacher, trainer and life coach who helps individuals cultivate peace and wholeness from the inside out. She is a professional speaker, meetings facilitator, and published author.

She resides in Southern Maryland where she enjoys spending time with her husband, two dogs, the outdoors, traveling and riding her motorcycle. Promoting and participating in social groups and gatherings based on health, wellness, healing, and spirituality is her favorite pastime.

It's Not What You
Think It Is

I t was after 6:00 p.m. I popped open my boss' door to tell him I was leaving for the day. Usually, I would have knocked because he meets with clients on a regular basis. It was late, and since he was, in fact, my newlywed husband, I guess I felt privileged to enter without forewarning. Much to my surprise, the crack of the opening door startled him and a woman I did not know. They abruptly turn their heads toward the door. They were sitting across from one another discussing private business matters. The unpredictable event caused a look of shock on their faces. I quickly apologized and said I was heading home for the day and shut the door.

Immediately, I began trembling. My mind was racing, and I felt overwhelmed with suspicion. My body was shaking with upset, and the certainty of his infidelity was building. I became angry, and my thoughts were spinning, "He's cheating. I knew it. I can't trust anyone. Those faces were a dead giveaway. I need a divorce." All this materialized in my head before I made it to my car. A small voice was in disbelief, "Wait Michéle, wait…what are you thinking? He was sitting across the table from her. He is a professional. It was completely innocent." My blood was beginning to boil with intensity. A part of me was convinced he had fooled around the entire relationship and commenced to dissect any interaction he'd had with a woman since we met.

I started my drive home with a hint of awareness. I was floored at the insanity taking over my system. I had practiced enough mindfulness to recognize this as the opportune time to be present with what is going on. The energy felt so real and concrete, even though I was well aware that my assessment was more than irrational. Less than a mile from the office, I pulled into a grocery store parking lot.

Tears poured down my face. I was terrified to feel the fury. Something else inside me knew if I didn't stop the crazy thoughts and feel what was happening within my body, the neurotic force was going to take over, and most likely ruin my marriage. It felt extreme. My body was in fight and flight at the same time. The mania felt uncontrollable. "Breathe, Michéle, breathe," said my inner teacher. "There is more going on than it seems. You are safe now. Breathe and let yourself feel." I started to calm, a little. Wild conjecture kept trying to grab me, "Go home and pack your bags, run as far away as you can." I shifted my attention numerous times to return to feeling my body. There was energy in motion (e-motion) even though I wasn't physically moving. It was uncomfortable, yet I was willing to trust that love was somehow beneath the fear. Once again, my brain screamed, trying to convince me I was in danger. "Thank you,'" I said with sincerity, and returned my focus to feeling, really feeling. My jaw tense, my guts churning, and a short intense energy moving like a jackhammer on concrete pounded my core. I breathed, finally giving myself enough space to relax into the un-comfortableness of it all.

A movie gently appeared on the screen of my mind. I was walking down a hallway and approached a wooden door, similar, but different to that at my husband's office. The pop as I opened the door jolted two people apart from a passionate kiss, quickly retrieving hands from each other's body. The man was my boyfriend of three years and the woman a long-time friend. It was a memory with stuck emotion from 15 years prior. Back then, I pretended I didn't see it and acted as if nothing happened. It felt safer that way. I ignored the pattern of betrayal for many years, relationship after relationship, until I ended them all out of fear. My inner protector became hypervigilant to make sure I didn't get the wool pulled over my eyes again.

Finally, I chose to get healthy. I learned to transform my thoughts and changed a load of beliefs. I manifested a healthy, stable, monogamous man into my life. What I hadn't done was *feel* my way through the old layers of betrayal and hurt. When those sores were lightly touched, my protector came out in full force. Being present to truly honor and experience the fears of my inner world seemed risky. Yet, it was the very thing my heart required to be free. The awareness to distinguish the subtle variations of thought, vision, emotion, the physical body and that of spirit, gave me another layer of healing.

My body instantly melted in a pool of relief and understanding. Today's experience was not that old movie. Intellectually, I knew I didn't catch my husband cheating, but everything else in my body screamed otherwise. It felt so real. The sounds and pictures of hurtful scenes of the past had been recorded in my heart. My natural defenses were triggered to respond. If I had tried to push away the panic or pretend it wasn't there, like I had so many times before, it would have won. I am grateful because those same fight and flight defenses took good care of me when I needed it, betrayal after betrayal. This was not that. I am a transformed person now. A smile of admiration hijacked my face. The newly-released old movie made so much sense. It allowed the extreme irrational thought to finally retire. Balance could be restored.

The language of the heart is boundless. It may communicate with words, pictures, feelings, a sense, a nudge, or something else. It offers messages in many ways and at the same time operates within the confines of human perception. Expanding the ability to be fully present requires a deepening of relationship with the co-creative aspects of oneself: thinking mind, visual mind, physical body, body of emotion, and spirit.

One of my teachers, Hu Dalconzo, taught me the Spiritual Distinction Meditation (SDM). SDM is the first interactive meditation that helped me build a two-way relationship with these aspects. There are three phases. The first phase is breathing, becoming present, and connecting with the feeling of the breath. Phase two is a shift in mindfulness to perceive the senses: hearing, smelling, tasting, and the sensitive touch of the skin. I concentrate with each sense one at a time. I fully experience it before moving to the next one. Phase three is the distinction phase. I practice feeling the difference between my physical body and my breath. Next, I notice the commonalities and disparities of my physical body and the visual imagery in my mind. Shifting focus to my thinking mind, I feel how thought energy and the energy of the breath contrast. Lastly, I breathe rapidly a handful of times and bond with the expanded sense of Self. It can be helpful to make a list of these steps to follow until the process becomes automatic.

Being gentle with myself is an important part of the process. This is a practice to experience and grow, not a perfection game. Practice this daily and you are guaranteed to have greater recognition and response to your intuitive heart whispers. All messages need your love and inter-active consciousness. There are those that need to be recognized and released back into the past, and those that provide direction for the future. Understanding the distinction opens the pathway of intuition. The gift, of course, is living in the present.

Dedicated to my husband, Jeff Quesenberry, for always being so patient and loving. I love you with all my heart.

Many friends, teachers, coaches and counselors have encouraged my personal healing and professional growth over the years. To all of you, I have much gratitude. I would particularly like to thank Hu Dalconzo for his tenacity and creativity in teaching me to holistically care for my body, mind and spirit.

~ Michéle Hatfield Quesenberry

Deanna Leigh

DEANNA LEIGH is a seasoned C-Level executive with 30 years of experience. She was dedicated and determined to climb the corporate ladder making tough decisions quickly, being a leader, and always demonstrating confidence to excel.

Her diverse background from Not-For-Profit, Corporate, Higher Education, and Governmental management positions, ranges from Director to Chief Financial Officer.

She has a family history of military service which includes — Marines, Navy, Air Force, and Army. Her life has been richly blessed with unforgettable life experiences by living all over the world and experiencing other cultures.

After going through a life-changing event, she purposely began a quest for self-discovery and became a strong advocate in helping others do the same. She is passionate about helping people, sharing her life lessons, being a voice for women, and inspiring everyone she meets.

She is a published author, international writer, public speaker, and sought-after business consultant.

info@deanna-leigh.com
www.deanna-leigh.com

Life is About Choices

I believe that everyone comes to a point in their lives when they look back and ask themselves important questions regarding the choices they've made. After all, our life is a series of choices. We make decisions all day long, without really giving it much thought. Our choices are either wise or not so wise. Right? Sometimes we simply aren't choosing wisely based on past experiences or beliefs we might have. Nevertheless, all of us are aware that our choices do matter.

Let me give you an example of how important a choice is whether it be conscious or unconscious, may change the course of your journey. I often think about the people who were saved from the terrible tragedy on 9/11 when the twin towers in New York City were struck by terrorists that morning. Most of us can still recall what we were doing or where we were when we first heard the news. It was an event none of us, here and abroad, will ever forget. The whole world was affected. I remember hearing some reports awhile later about individuals who were saved that day for surprising reasons. One woman didn't feel well, so she called in sick very early that morning and went back to bed, unaware of what transpired until later. Another person over slept because she forgot to set her alarm the night before. One man missed his usual train because he had to take the kids to school, then he forgot something at home and went back to get it. I could go on and on with more accounts of folks whose direction changed that day. None of them knew that those little things would change their life's path forever.

Some of you might think those were coincidences, but quite frankly, I don't believe in coincidences. I believe that everything comes into existence for a reason, no matter if it's good or not good. Take you for instance, you are reading this book for a reason, whether you realize it or not. There is something in my story or another writer's narrative that you are meant to read! There is a message in this book somewhere for you. I say that without hesitation or doubt!

As for me, I am no different than anyone else in regards to looking back on my life. I was in my early thirties when my time came. I was devastated going through a divorce with two small children who were looking to me to be their rock and source of everything — me not knowing what I was going to do. My ex-husband simply walked away because he didn't want a wife and children anymore. I had to get my ducks in a row quickly! I remember sitting down after putting the little ones to bed one night, feeling extremely tired, I began to cry. It was in this brokenness that I began to ask myself:

> *"What part did I play in this divorce and being so broken?"*
> *"What is my purpose in life?"*
> *"What gives me joy?"*
> *"Am I being a good parent?"*
> *"Am I spiritually growing?"*
> *"If I weren't afraid, what would I do right now without hesitation?"*
> *"Where do I begin to get my life where I want it to be?"*

When you ask yourself these BIG questions out loud, your subconscious delivers the answer to your mind. The very first thought received is your answer. Our minds run like the internet on our computer. When you ask a question, it delivers a response, if there is one. You must be quiet and very still to hear it. Now that you have the solution, it's up to you to act up on it or dismiss it. Again that is a choice.

Typically when this occurs, something has triggered a feeling inside you to start asking deep questions. Some people perceive this as a "mid-life" crisis, which is not always a bad thing. I don't think the word "crisis" is the right word to use. I view it as a deep "awakening." I think that term better describes what's taking place. I am very grateful I was awakened on a deeper level in that moment and the days following that night.

When you hear of someone going through a "mid-life crisis," you tend to think of a man. Men are usually attached to those words to a greater extent than women. Men might show it more visibly because they sometimes make drastic changes in their lives. They may suddenly after 20 years get divorced and buy a new, shiny red sports car that makes them feel alive again! I bet this guy asked himself the question, "If I weren't afraid, what would I do right now without hesitation?" And the first answer that came to his mind was, "Get divorced." He was probably unhappy in his marriage for a very long time but never wanted to be divorced; so he remained married despite his unhappiness. He may have stayed because he loved his youngsters so deeply, but not his wife. Friends and family around him might perceive this as a drastic change. But you know what, I'm proud of anyone who is finally awakened and stands up to living the truth — their organic and true reality. Because this is their life, their world, their euphoria and their personal bliss. Kudos to them for stepping out of their comfort zone, making a huge decision to be happy and choosing the genuineness they want to live going forward. Those are BIG life-altering choices!

What about your choices? What would you do if you weren't afraid? Pause for a moment and ask yourself that question. What answer first came to your mind when you asked?

Personally, I decided in my brokenness to go back to college and finish my degree. I knew when the answer came to me that I would need to support my little ones on my own without my husband's help. The only way I could do that effectively and with less stress would be to finish my Bachelor's Degree. So with two small kids, recently divorced, no money, and only a deep desire to provide for my babies, I went back to college in my thirties.

The next two years would be a blur. I worked part-time, attended courses full-time, and took care of my children. I got up early to get them ready for daycare. I was blessed to know the woman who owned the daycare in our small town because she was part of my church family. She gave me a small break on daycare cost by volunteering one shift a week. A lot of the teachers there went to our church so the kids felt very comfortable and loved. I knew they were well taken care of while I was spending so many hours working at the university and going to class.

I had to be very structured to get this accomplished. I was also very determined. After finishing my job and school, I'd swing by to pick up my darlings from daycare. We'd go home and I'd let them play, as I fixed something easy for dinner. We'd eat and talk about their day. Who got in trouble and what happened on the playground. You know, all the important stuff to them. Then, we'd do bath time. That was the fun part. We'd laugh as I'd sit on the floor next to the tub, because we'd play the soap on the back — guess the letter game. It was all part of "our time." Then I'd get them ready for bed, including brushing their teeth. We'd say our prayers, give lots of kisses, and lights out by 8:30 P.M. I'd go finish the kitchen cleanup and then head to the table to do my homework. I'd finish up by 11:00 P.M., then it was out for me. This was our routine Monday — Friday without fail because structure was a part of our success.

Graduation day finally came! WooHoo!! It was a magnificent day. My whole family drove in from another state to see me walk across the stage to accept my diploma. I now had achieved my Bachelor's Degree in Business from the University. No one else in my family or even my parent's generation had ever graduated from college. This was a monumental moment for both sides of my family. My kids witnessed this remarkable event with great happiness as my relatives celebrated along with me this huge accomplishment. To this day, my children still remember this event. It's something we talk about often and how difficult that time was for me, but I overcame the adversity because of my determination.

As I look back on the day my ex-husband came into the room to ask me for a divorce, I remember feeling broken, helpless, confused and saddened that my marriage failed. I even hated him for doing this! How could he abandon his offspring? I didn't know how I would make it through and stand alone with two babies who were solely counting on me. But what's truly astonishing and phenomenal, was I also had no idea I was about to discover the gift he, in fact, gave me that day! The gift was "an incredible life" moving forward. I didn't have to struggle anymore with someone who didn't love me. I could SOAR with wings of eagles in the world that I was destined to live.

True — every choice gives you a chance to pave your own road! The divorce wasn't my choice, but his. He was being true to himself and what he wanted for his life and in that choice, it allowed him to give a gift to me. If we are true to who we are, that certainly can't be wrong.

I've learned that with every pain comes great purpose. It is in the pain or the storms of life we experience personal growth and enlightenment. If our history didn't have the hills and valleys, we'd be numb to love, joy, happiness, laughter, and heartbreak. The pain allows us to break free and experience great joy, great love, great happiness, wonderful laughter and sometimes sorrow.

I've learned that life is to be lived according to YOU — not anyone else. Be true to who you are. You may be different. You may not fit in right now. But what I do know is this — one day you will fit in. One day you will find out why God made you different, if you don't already know. One day you will find the one true love who loves all those unique qualities that you possess. And one day is just around the corner. Be true to who you are. It's the only way you will ever find your bliss. Life is best when you are jubilant inside your heart.

I've learned that God gives us strength if we just ask. I never dreamed I'd accomplish so much. It was in the brokenness that I asked for God's strength and discernment for my life! I leaned on him and loved ones around me for moral support. When we are weak, we gather strength and love from those around us. Let me also share this with you: after receiving my degree, I labored hard to climb to the top of the corporate world as a CFO, Chief Financial Officer. Not many women can claim that! But I can. And if I can do it, so can you. God can do wonders — transforming a broken heart!

In closing, let me share this about our choices. You must be mindful of what you want for yourself. You must know who you are and love yourself right here and now! If you don't have a clue, then make time to figure it out. Ask yourself the important questions now. Write down your answers. Every choice gives you a chance to pave your own road, but it helps to know what direction you want to go. And with that comes responsibility. If you want to soar on wings like eagles, then make wise choices. But if you don't make a wise choice today, remember every morning gives you a fresh start!

I heard Oprah say this recently before I began my morning meditation:

> *"Every choice begins with intention.*
> *Your intentions create thoughts.*
> *Your thoughts create choices.*
> *And your choices create your life!"*

Make your life AMAZING! Make it WITHOUT apologies and regrets. It's your choice.

Dedicated to God, foremost, for giving me strength and confidence. To my angels for surrounding me in love and healing. And to Aubrey, Andrew, Adyson Leighann, Dexter Scott, and David Andrew — you are my greatest joys!

A very special thank you for my followers, family, and friends who love me with all my scars, completely support my purpose, and are there for me along on my journey. Each one of you are a blessing!

I thank God for every life experience thus far. I believe it has given me more compassion and understanding. My heart is truly grateful for all my spiritual gifts. My intentions will be in sharing my gifts.

~ Deanna Leigh

Carole Cassell

CAROLE CASSELL is a licensed Heal Your Life® Coach, workshop leader, certified health coach, and licensed massage therapist. Carole is passionate about helping others transform their lives by connecting to their spirit and soul so they may heal from past wounds and live a life of divine guidance. Carole's unique set of skills allows her to help clients conquer chaos, create clarity, and cultivate health by addressing the whole person — mind, body, and spirit. A proud Mom to D.J. and Zach, and wife to Roger. Carole treasures her family and enjoys every moment in their presence!

www.carolecassell.com

Ready or Not

The Vision

"Oh my gosh — did you see that?" I ask excitedly, as I look over at my husband Roger.

"No, but I could tell something was happening to you — where did you go?"

It's a beautiful spring day and the sun shines brightly, illuminating the dust particles floating through the air. The warmth it generates radiates through our windows, so badly in need of replacing.

Roger sits on the floor, one leg bent, his elbow resting on his other knee, as he leans back against the left end of the couch. I sit Indian style on the loveseat facing him, as we catch up after his recent long business trip. The television in the background projects soundless images, muted, as our conversation has become all encompassing. We're in the flow of one of those awesomely wonderful conversations, both fully immersed, present, and in sync.

Suddenly, what looks like a mini-movie screen drops down between us and what appears to be *my future* begins to play out before my eyes! Sort of like one of those *This Is Your Life* scenes from a movie.

Wait, where am I? My mind races to make sense of what's happening when I hear a whisper: *Just sit back, relax, and look at what's in store for you.* This whisper isn't foreign to me, but it's one I haven't heard in quite a while. Though initially I fight the urge to figure out what's happening, I acquiesce quickly to the whisper's request and allow myself to stay fully present with the vision before me.

What I see is breathtaking! At first, it's like I'm flying just above the treetops over a beautiful piece of property deep in the woods. Rolling hills, lush green grass, and absolute beauty as far as my eyes can see. The next thing I know I'm in the back of a limo, being driven up one of those rolling hills. I gaze in awe, eager to see what's next. My heart begins to pound as the car slows, then turns right and makes its way down a long, winding, artistically-paved driveway.

Where am I going? I wonder. Just as that question enters my mind, I gasp as the car comes upon a clearing that opens to a *whole other world … a world designed specifically for healing!* The tour continues and I'm shown every building, every garden, and the beautiful babbling brook that runs behind this property. Overcome with a sense of excitement, yet a feeling of peace, there's a *knowing* that this is indeed my future!

Best of all, I see exactly which services I'll be offering here, and what I'm going to learn in order to make all of this happen. No longer in accounting, but instead trained in massage therapy, holistic health coaching, Reiki, and aromatherapy — I glimpse my future self as a spiritual teacher who helps others strengthen their internal relationship to *self,* and thus improve their relationships with others.

Suddenly, as quickly as it arrived, the mini-movie screen vanishes and I'm back in the living room with Roger. *What the heck just happened?* I muse, as it takes me a moment to get my bearings. *Why would this happen to me — of all people? I've never desired to be any of those things! This has to be some weird daydream. It can't truly be a vision … can it?*

I spend the rest of the afternoon describing to Roger what I just witnessed. His eyes dance with wonderment as I share with him this most amazing journey and how every detail — from light fixtures to stepping stones — was revealed to me! We talk about what this could mean.

Roger and I are logical people, after all. We don't believe in visions, we believe in *facts*. I mean, look at us, my incredibly intelligent, grounded husband with his PhD in organic chemistry, and me, a corporate controller who's spent her entire life working to achieve that position.

However, this afternoon we sit, caught up in this vision of mine, called to suspend our disbelief long enough to entertain this idea as a potential reality — for the moment at least.

Back to Reality

As the sun rises the next day, life resumes as usual. Roger returns to his lab and I to my office. We speak about my vision off and on, and it's delicious to recall the wonderfully-alive energy of it, but it's not long before it makes its way into the background of our thoughts. To quote a dear friend of mine, we are, of course, "busy and important" in the lives we've created.

However, try as I might, my life never actually returns to *normal*. In fact, a bit of the opposite happens. The job I love becomes even more demanding and I grow increasingly unhappy. Something inside starts to feel as if I'm being unfaithful … *to myself.*

Many times I leave work miserable. I sit on the couch in the evenings wondering what's happening. Each time, Spirit urges me to begin my training in the healing arts, so I'll be ready when the location of my vision is revealed to me.

Initially, I muster every ounce of resistance I can — I mean, come on, I've worked my entire life to obtain the corporate position I have now! Plus, I'm making more money than ever before! Why would I give that up? In addition, Roger and I are just getting back on our feet after a few financial setbacks, so how can I even think of walking away from the security we've worked so hard to build? This is all so crazy and illogical!

Nope, it's not going to happen! I protest defiantly. Again and again, I ask God why I'm being called to make these changes and the only answer I ever hear is — *follow your vision!*

Then I think back to the connection and passion I felt when first meeting Roger, I just knew he was *the one.* My decision to leave the life I had to go with him definitely wasn't based on logic — matter of fact it was one of the most illogical decisions I've ever made and caused much chaos and disruption in my life. However, I wouldn't be with the right man now if I'd listened to my head only and ignored my heart. I begin to toy with the idea that perhaps it's time once again to favor my heart over my head. Maybe there really *is* something to this idea!

Finally, after several months of this inner turmoil, I throw my hands into the air and yell to the heavens, in a rather bratty way, *"Fine! I hear you! I'll do it! I'll follow my vision!"* Instantly, I feel a release of worry, tension, and turmoil. While no trumpets play or angels sing and still I experience trepidation, a strange sense of peace descends and settles within.

And So It Begins

"I think you should do it, babe, it just feels right!" is Roger's response when I call him to discuss how he feels about my going forward to make my vision into a reality. *I can't believe it!* My chemist, my man who deals in provable concepts, fully supportive of me embarking on a new career with only *a vision* as a guide?

Immediately, I begin researching massage schools in my area. The second one I visit is *the one.* I know it from the moment I pull into the parking lot. I sit patiently through the presentation waiting to find out how much it's going to cost me, and just about tip over in my chair when they finally reveal the total school fee of $10,000! That, and two days a week away from my job! My head spins! Not ready yet to *trust* Spirit fully, I start to panic.

Roger and I are already in debt, where am I going to find that kind of money?

Within two days, my answer arrives. I open my mailbox to find an offer for 0% APR on all purchases for three years from a credit card company I'd used back in the early 90's.

Impossible! I call the credit card company to verify the offer's validity. I still remember the amazement in the voice of the customer service rep as she looks up my account.

"I've never seen an offer like this in all my years here, but yes, Mrs. Cassell, that is a valid offer," she tells me. I share with her a bit of my vision and we marvel at the power of God, both knowing full well this offer was orchestrated by a higher power.

I hang up the phone and immediately break down in tears. *Is this truly happening?* Fear and insecurity start to rear their ugly heads and the battle between my heart and my head begins to rage.

Who am I to think I have anything to offer people? This vision defies logic — and I deal solely with logic! I should stick to what I know! When I ask myself *why should I start over?* the tears flow even harder, as once again I hear the whisper from Spirit urging me simply to *trust.*

And for the first time…I do! Immediately I'm filled with a *knowing* that this truly is the right path and — logical or not — it marks the beginning of the shift in my belief in this journey.

Massage school starts in October, 2009, and I love it, most of the time. It proves daunting about six months later when I begin to struggle with traversing two worlds: my logical corporate job, and an environment that deals with energy, intention, and a belief in things you can't *see.* In addition, I'm still a mother and wife and need to take care of my son and Roger!

The toll on me mounts, and Roger, my biggest cheerleader, urges me to quit my job.

"No way!" I protest. "How can we give up my income and still make it?" He reminds me that something much bigger is at play, and assures me we'll be okay — somehow. Deep down I know he's right, and recognize once more the battle between my head and my heart.

I give notice the next day and Spirit comes through again, as if on cue, when Roger's boss calls him in to inform him of a raise. Outside of normal raise time, no less! This helps ease our financial burden. Two months later Roger receives a large bonus and we're able to pay off some of our debt, which allows us to live on his income alone. Finally, we can breathe!

A true believer now, I consult with Spirit about my every move. *When should I begin my holistic health coach training?* I ask, and hear, "one year after you start your massage business." I finish massage school and am divinely-guided to a location I can rent for my practice. I sign my lease, hang my shingle, and get to work. Within one year I have no shortage of clients, am financially secure, and ready to begin my next training.

Just as before, I open my mailbox to find *another* offer from the same credit card company, and once again am able to finance my education for 0% interest! I'm rich now in the knowing that, as long as I trust the guidance from within and follow the path laid out for me in my vision, all my needs will be met.

I receive my certification as a holistic health coach and begin to tackle the other trainings shown to me in my vision. I become a Level III Reiki practitioner, receive my certification in aromatherapy, and am ordained as a minister, so I can work with others in a spiritual capacity.

This latter path gives me pause. *What on earth do I have to offer people in the way of spirituality?* The old insecurities arise and yet another battle ensues between my head and my heart. I'm about as far from religious as you can get! However, I *have* developed a strong spiritual practice since this journey began — a practice that has strengthened my relationship with God and with myself, and improved *all* the relationships in my life! *Is that what I'm meant to help people with?* I wonder.

I turn to Spirit for answers and am reminded immediately of Louise Hay's *You Can Heal Your Life* books, which assisted me in moving past so many issues related to both my health and my marriage to Roger, and reminded me of the love I have for God. Just like before, I'm washed over with a knowing that this is the right path. *I can do this! I can help other people learn to listen to the messages of their spirit*! After all, that's what I've been doing for the past four years!

I begin researching how I can become a teacher of Louise Hay's work and run across a husband and wife team who, with Louise, developed a training and licensing program. I pick up the phone to find that the last training of the year is being held only a few short weeks away in California. I sign up immediately, make my arrangements, and become a licensed Heal Your Life® Teacher, Coach and Workshop leader in October, 2014.

Living My Purpose

Now that I've learned to trust the messages of my heart, I know my purpose is to assist others to connect to their spirit and their soul, so they may heal from past wounds and live a life of divine guidance. Through my Heal Your Life® workshops and online programs I have the pleasure of watching people from all walks of life transform their lives. As they strengthen their relationships with themselves and those they love, they heal all types of issues — physical, emotional, and spiritual.

As I look back now from a place of peace, stability, and spiritual connection, I realize how many years my heart battled with my head. Grateful for the lessons I learned throughout this process, my life now is better than I could have ever imagined! I have a career I am passionate about, my marriage is amazing, and my new relationship with Spirit permeates my entire being.

I thank God on a regular basis that Spirit did not desert me, but rather taught me how to be a warrior in the battle against a dynamic duo — my logical mind and the societal expectations to which I once fell victim.

Now that I've learned to confidently walk the path of my spirit, I look forward to the day the location in my vision is revealed to me. I don't know when that will happen, or where it will be, I only know that I'll be ready when it does!

Dedicated to those of you for whom the battle rages often between your head and your heart — may my story connect you to your own inner knowing, and bring forth the courage to follow the whispers of your heart.

Thanks to my incredibly supportive husband Roger, and my sons D.J. and Zach, for sticking by me through all the times I reinvented myself, and for your unwavering belief in me throughout this process. A special thanks to you, Mom! You've believed in me since the day you held me in yours arms and, even more, through the times when my decisions didn't make sense to anyone but me. Your never-ending faith in me, coupled with your unconditional love, drove me even harder to live the life we both knew was my destiny. I could not love you more!

~ Carole Cassell

Cheryl Guttenberg

CHERYL GUTTENBERG is a licensed Heal Your Life® Coach and workshop leader, healer, author and speaker. As a Vice President of Human Resources, she is able to teach people how to empower themselves and to live a happy and healthy life in the corporate world. She also assists individuals through her workshops and coaching practice.

Cheryl has also coached executives to achieve the life of their dreams and create a good work/life balance.

Cheryl lives in Southern California and enjoys traveling, spending time with her family and escaping to the dance floor as often as possible.

CherylGuttenberg.com
CherylGuttenberg@gmail.com

Remember to Dance

The Perfect Picture

When I was in my late 30s, I can recall visualizing how my life would be in my 60s. My house would be paid in full, my husband and I would have accumulated sufficient retirement savings, we'd be taking our grown children and their families on annual vacations, and we would travel. Since I loved to dance, I would definitely take lessons and dance whenever I had the opportunity to do so.

Life Happens While You're Making Plans

Upon reaching my 60s, however, my life wasn't exactly as I had envisioned it. In fact, it couldn't have been any further away from what I had planned. I found myself going through a divorce, moving out of my beautiful home, starting over financially, and losing my best friend to breast cancer. And I had just been laid off from the management position I had held for nine years. My entire world had been turned upside down. Now what? I was feeling lost, afraid, and full of anxiety. At my age, I had to rebuild my entire life.

When I found myself bombarded with these deep and seemingly insurmountable life changes, I wasn't sure where to begin. During the past ten years I had gotten serious about my spiritual growth and had sought out great teachers such as Louise Hay, Deepak Chopra, Wayne Dryer, Cheryl Richardson, Bryon Katie, and Dr. Patricia Crane, among many others. I attended several *I Can Do It* conferences, which featured several other gifted teachers. It was now time for me to put on my big girl pants and rely on myself to use the tools I had acquired to get myself through this. I needed to trust the Universe. Being hit with so much at one time, it wasn't easy. In my heart, I knew that the key to overcoming my problems would be to simply trust life.

First and foremost, I needed to find my own place to live. I had moved many times in the recent past due to separating and reconciling with my husband, and felt this should be the top priority on my "to do" list. I set an intention on finding my perfect new home. My ideal new place would be in a good neighborhood, a quiet area, good location for future job commute, and a place I felt safe. I got in my car and asked the Universe for direction and assistance in finding my new home. On the first street I drove down, I noticed a sign for a one bedroom loft apartment. I parked my car and called the manager. She was a charming older woman from Russia. We had an immediate connection and I moved into my beautiful new apartment three weeks later.

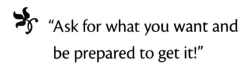 "Ask for what you want and
be prepared to get it!"

~ MAYA ANGELOU

What's Next?

The next order of business was to find a job. The next nine months were spent networking, attending business meetings and sending out resumes. Although I had a few job interviews, no offers were forthcoming. Pessimistic thoughts were streaming through my mind: "Since I am in my 60s, and with so many people looking for a job, my age is against me. Maybe my career is just over, and if it is, what in the heck am I going to do? What's going to happen to me for the rest of my life?" I remember a two week period during which I was filled with depression and negativity. I knew this type of thinking was not going to get me the results I was seeking and that I needed to change my thinking. Louise Hay's words were in my head: "When you change your thoughts, you change your life." I went back to my mirror work and also got serious about writing my affirmations every day. I started visualizing how it would feel to work at a full-time job which I loved.

 "If you change the way you look at things,
the things you look at change."

~ WAYNE DYER

A few weeks later while driving out of town with a good friend, my phone rang. It was a woman who worked for me at a previous job. She was leaving her Human Resources Director position and asked if I'd be interested in taking it. The only drawback was it was a part-time job. But after being out of work for nine months with no other job offers, this sounded pretty good to me, and the following week I started my new job. Working at a job where I was able to make a difference in the employees' work lives, I was living my passion. However, I wasn't enjoying being a department of one without a staff to coach and mentor. A few months later, I began to feel that I had accomplished everything there I was supposed to, and that my time with this employer was coming to an end. I needed to trust and turn this over to the Universe and go dancing! Over the last 20 years, I've spent a lot of time on the dance floor. I love it all—swing, Latin, ballroom, freestyle. There is nothing like listening to the music and letting your body interpret what you hear. Nothing else matters . . .

In working with my daily affirmations, I made the decision to describe my perfect new job. I wanted to work for a solvent company with good benefits whose management really believed and acknowledged that their employees are their best asset, have a staff to work with, and where I could really make a difference.

One afternoon at work, I received an email from a list serve professional group I was a member of, stating that there was a company seeking a new Vice President of Human Resources to replace the retiring VP. This was a stable company located only six miles from my home, with an HR staff of five. I responded immediately and requested a copy of the job description, which validated that I was a perfect candidate for this job! Within a week I was meeting with the VP. She asked me when I could start, if selected for the position. I told her I needed to give a two week notice and would like to take off a week in between jobs. She said that worked well for her and she would be making a hiring decision the following week. I left the interview having a great feeling about the position and a strong sense that the job would be mine.

 "Ask the Universe for what you want. Don't worry about the details or how it will unfold, sit back and watch what happens. This is real trust."

~ CHERYL GUTTENBERG

New Beginnings

That evening I saw a Facebook post from Louise Hay regarding a *Heal Your Life®* Workshop training, based upon her teachings. "I have to do this, I was meant to do this." I didn't know where or when the training was offered or the cost, but I had a distinct and clear message I was supposed to attend. After further research, I discovered the training would take place in San Diego in three weeks, and would last for a week. "If I get the new job and find out next week, I can give my notice and the training will fall on the week in between the jobs." Just in case it didn't happen like I was projecting it would, the next day at work I submitted a request for vacation for that week. The following week I was offered the new job and submitted my two week notice. The workshop indeed fell on my week off between jobs. Putting out an intention and allowing the Universe to figure out the details really works.

I was so excited about my new job at this wonderful organization where I would have a staff to coach and mentor. I was getting all I wanted when I affirmed my ideal job! My life was really starting to fall into place perfectly. The following week, I received a voicemail from the VP whom I would be replacing at the new company. I was worried for a moment that something was wrong. When I called her back, she asked me how I was and said she would be increasing my starting salary by $5,000 per year. Who does that?? My life just kept getting better and better. Time to go dancing . . .

 "Our deepest fear is not that we are inadequate. Our deepest fear is that we are powerful beyond measure."

~ MARIANNE WILLIAMSON

Attending the week long workshop training was a transformative time for me. It was an opportunity to learn more about myself and release some things that were no longer serving me. I met many wonderful people, who like myself, were on their spiritual journey and wanting to help others by showing and giving them tools to live their best life.

Living My Life Purpose

Many years ago, I recall watching an Oprah program that was about finding your life purpose. At the time I asked myself, "What is my life purpose?" I didn't revisit this until many years later, but when I did, I was surprised at what I discovered. My life purpose is to help others to heal so they can live their best life. What a shock when I realized that I had already been doing this for the past 20 years through the Human Resources management positions which I had held, and by coaching those around me. Now that I am a certified Heal Your Life® workshop leader and coach, I can reach even more people. Life is good . . . it's time to go dancing.

 "When you dance, your purpose is not to
get to a certain place on the dance floor.
It's to enjoy each step along the way."

~ WAYNE DYER

To my dear friend Jenny ~ I miss you so much and think about you every day and know you are with me daily. You were taken away from us far too soon. I acknowledge the numerous roles you played in my life. In the beginning, you were my boss, then my friend, my spiritual mentor and ultimately my best friend and soul twin sister. The world is a better place because you were here. You touched everyone's heart you came in contact with.

Thank you, Universe for teaching me I can live the life of my dreams and can stretch myself to achieve things I never would have thought I could.

~ Cheryl Guttenberg

Tonia Browne

TONIA BROWNE is a nurturer of young minds, whatever the age of the body. As a qualified teacher, Tonia has worked in the United Kingdom and internationally for over twenty years and was an Assistant Head for six. She is a Heal Your Life® Workshop Leader, Coach and Business Trainer. Tonia is a strong advocate of inviting fun into our lives and encouraging people to see that there is MORE out there. She is a Usui Reiki and an Angelic Reiki Master, who is also qualified in Spiritual Life Coaching, Colour Therapy, Oracle Card Reading, Facial Reflexology and more.

toniabrowne@hotmail.com
toniabrowne.com
facebook.com/Time4Tonia

🌿 Rag Doll Blues!

"**N**ever give up on yourself."

"Be willing to believe, be willing to seek and be willing to hear."

"Know you are worth it; for you are a child of the universe and by merely existing you are loved."

(These words continue to whisper to my heart as treasures from past books and workshops. I hope they can comfort and inspire you too. ~Tonia Browne)

I Can, I Can, I Can

My mother hugged me. "You did it! If only your old headmaster was here, I'd tell him, I'd show him your Masters Degree!" she whispered. "No-one should write a child off that early, no-one!" she said, somewhat louder. "It only seems like yesterday he told me you would not get any kind of qualification!" she sniffed, before giving me one of her beautiful smiles.

If only I had known earlier about the amazing information and ways of thinking shared by the inspirational Louise Hay and her Hay House authors, I would have known that whatever my headmaster thought of me was *none of my business*. I was not limited to his perception of who I could be. If I had not jumped so easily into believing his prophesy, my early life might have been different, and the emotional pain I gave to my parents reduced. Instead, it was years of tears as a child, and years of *not playing* as an adult.

My journey of self-empowerment helped me discover a hurt and stubborn little child dwelling within me. This *inner child* was holding the reigns of my life and limiting my options, due to her fear of failure. With strategies to appease and comfort her now in place, I have made peace with myself. This allows me to enjoy the day so much more. I can now say with much conviction *"I can, I can, I can!"*

Before We Met

It was around the age of forty when my deep self-exploration really began. I no longer saw myself as this humorous and independent soul, but rather an odd and undeserving thing who shunned any kind of serious relationship to prevent herself from being shunned first. I did not feel good enough. It was around this time that I made my request to the universe to step in and help. Surely there could be more; surely I could step up!

Outwardly, I was doing alright. I had qualifications, a career and some good people in my life. This was quite remarkable considering I had failed the 11-plus exam. I was initially placed in the D stream at a secondary modern school and not the grammar school where my friends were. If my recollections are right, I was the only girl in that class. I was a child who still spluttered her words after sessions of speech therapy, who found reading a challenge and found social interactions all too stressful. My primary headmaster had called my mother in to share his views that some children were academic and went on to do rewarding and amazing things, and others were practical, and they too could go on to achieve and have fulfilling lives. However, there were some children who would do neither. What could they possibly go on to do? He did not have answers.

My mother did. She moved as soon as she could to her hometown, which had a system of education that did not believe in segregating children on academic ability so young. I was accepted into a local comprehensive school. She refused to believe the speech therapist's opinion that my speech might never improve and I would never easily be understood. She gave me speech therapy sessions herself.

Looking back, with the knowledge I have today, I had learning needs, possibly a bit of attention deficit disorder, a smattering of language delay and almost certainly dyslexia. It was, however, what I heard and how I was treated that had the most detrimental effect. However much my mother would tell me she would not give up on me and that I just marched to a different drummer, I allowed others to make me feel unworthy. I felt different, misunderstood and I internalised that as being a failure.

Children in school who feel like this often respond in one of two ways: disruption or withdrawal. It is usually about control. I wanted the thumps on the table, the shouts in the ear to stop. I equated any request that I found challenging to process as being something that I should instantly burst into tears over. At least that way they left me in exasperation and stopped demanding answers. Hence, from a very early age I disengaged. This, initially, was an effective strategy for reducing pain. If I was their failure, then I refused to play their game! Thirty years on and the strategy was not so good. Life can be an amazing game and it is an honour to play. By disengaging I was serving no-one.

It was not that I did not know things. I did. They were just not what I was meant to know. When a teacher asked me what 4 x 9 was, I would look at them and see an emotional trail around their face. This may have been a vision of their early morning argument, the bills that had not been paid or the love that had not been reciprocated. Such circumstances resulted in pain and stress for them, which I could see congealing in a physical spot somewhere in their body and pulsating as a warning sign for some future medical attention. It was like a TV scene, far more compelling than engaging the necessary cortexes required to answer the mathematical sum.

At home the phone would ring and on occasions I could clearly see the person on the other end of the line, even though we might have never met. I knew the reason for their call before they even spoke. A child explores her world through honesty and vulnerability, but the shutters go down if you believe that something is not *right* or not *normal*. I shut down many of these gifts, and now I strive to reactivate them. It was only after my *inner child* work that I became more aware of how I approached life and how my emotional responses and thought patterns were preventing positive engagement in many areas of my adult life.

Getting Together

Some say life begins at forty and it was around this time that I gave out a strong request for another way to be. With some gentle whispers of the heart, the co-ordinates for a direct and beautiful collision with Louise Hay were set for me. These co-ordinates were to change my life for the better. It may have seemed to have taken longer than was necessary, but all is as it is meant to be in the *universal law of perfect timing*.

Through an amazing sequence of events I found myself traveling to Birmingham, England, for what would be a week of complete transformation. I had signed up for the Heal Your Life, Achieve your Dreams Workshop and left with the seeds for future growth firmly planted. This intense week with incredible people and access to inspirational ideas and strategies opened so many doors.

That gentle whisper that first made me curious and willing to seek became a powerful force, presenting opportunities to me — many before I knew I wanted them. The course showed me, amongst other things, how we respond as adults to emotionally-charged events with the same strategies that we did as a child. It introduced me to the concept of my *inner child*. We were encouraged to explore our early childhood and the child we were, and to find this still within us. We had the opportunity to acknowledge that this child still had control over our responses and hence over our lives.

I have to admit that the *inner child* work was not something I embraced immediately and probably resisted for some time. The other strategies were much more attractive; the meditation, the affirmations, the attention to language and the concept of consciousness were far easier for me to engage with. Yet that whisper persisted and eventually the heart heard and the body and mind took action.

I finally found my child huddled in a corner, head down, hugging a rag doll. Talk about Rag Doll Blues! She was unprepared to look up or to play. Change did not happen straight away, but the calling for another way was too strong to resist. With the light of love shining brightly from so many wonderful people and through words of support and encouragement, I coaxed the little child and that rag doll out of the corner — and we chatted.

After our initial meeting my *inner child* still retreated, but she was happier to explore, happier to try new things and was happier to connect more with others. Instead of fearing that people would suddenly shout and send her to the *dunce* corner or that she would be found wanting, she was more secure that she was doing the *best that she could*. Together we had a lot of fun — our type of fun.

It took a while longer to realise that my *inner child* was still quite a driving force in my life. I had wanted to show her that we could succeed in an institution that we believed wrote us off when we were young. At this time I was a Year Leader in a primary school. I wanted to play a small part in helping children not to choose the emotional response patterns *we* chose when *we* could not give what others expected. I wanted to be able to reassure some parents that life chances are not always decided so young. I had a greater opportunity to do this when I became an Assistant Head in a school, a school full of remarkable children and parents. It was a most rewarding chapter in my life. I knew we could not reach everyone, but we made a difference to some, and that was good.

My *inner child* still needed a lot of reassurance that the previous labels she was given were wrong, so I needed to show her that we could achieve academically if we wanted. I completed my Masters in Education and achieved it with a merit. My *inner child* was happy and as a reward she withdrew all her barriers to love. Recently, in my fifties, I have married an amazing man who has a big enough heart to love both of us. My mother cried with joy on both occasions. "It's your drum." she said. "It's always been your drum that you beat; it's only now that you let people hear the music."

Having made peace with my *inner child* I am able to play the game of life with more joy. She no longer sabotages my happiness, however unintentionally this may have been.

I would encourage anyone who feels that their life could be better to explore their *inner child* to ensure there is mutual support for the vision to change.

So What Next?

I will continue to check in with my *inner child*, but I am the adult now and she does not control my life in such a demanding way. I am creating a life I want rather than hiding from a life she did not want. I can take risks with relationships and can accept opportunities whether I succeed or fail. If anything, she adds that little bit of mischief and spontaneity that keeps life fun and surprising; like the time she caught sight of an opportunity to write a chapter in this book. "What fun it would be if the child who teachers found so hard to teach to read wrote her own chapter in a book!" she shared, smiling and waving her rag doll with such excitement.

And indeed it would!

Thanks to my family for always keeping a place in their hearts for me, to my friends who dance with me through this amazing journey called life. To Louise Hay and the phenomenal speakers and authors I have encountered on my learning quest, and to my husband and best friend, who showed me it was safe and wonderful to love.

Dedicated to the children in all of us — believe in them and let them play! Also dedicated to my father, R D Browne, who left this planet on 18th September 2012 but zooms in to support me still, as with the title of this book.

~ Tonia Browne

Michelle Reese

"There's got to be a better way," 9-year-old MICHELLE PREBILIC REESE believed. Today, as an author, wellness coach and workshop leader certified in Louise Hay's Heal Your Life® Program, she inspires adults and teens to throw out limiting beliefs and to create new life stories.

She lives in Walnut Creek, CA, where she enjoys her husband, adult children and friends. She's gone solar, nurtures a garden, rides a tandem, and shops for whole foods. She deeply appreciates Mt. Diablo for the healing nature and quiet it offers. She enjoys traveling throughout the world and embracing other cultures.

info@MichelleReese.com
MichelleReese.com

Our Disowned Superpowers

"Make it stop!" I silently screamed as my heart pounded erratically against my seven-year-old chest. "Make it stop!" I yelled silently to my heart, and my fear.

I had jolted awake full of anxiety and all I was aware of was the darkness and my pounding heart; my two younger sisters were still sleeping soundly in our bedroom. Then I heard it — slam, slam, slam! went the kitchen cabinets downstairs. I knew it was my Dad, and I knew something was wrong. I could feel his anger, irritation, and frustration. None of the other seven children in the household seemed to be hearing it. That scared me more!

I pulled the covers tightly up to my shoulders, even though I felt hot and sweaty. I wanted to hear him because I somehow felt responsible for whatever he was going through in that moment, and if I stopped listening, he wouldn't be okay.

The funny thing is, our kitchen occupied the back side of our four-bedroom, two-bath home. My bedroom, in the front of the two-story house, sat at the top of the stairs. I heard my Dad so clearly, as if he rummaged in the hallway right outside our bedroom. So how could a slam of a wooden kitchen cabinet travel so loudly through a formal dining room, up the stairs and through our closed bedroom door?

Kaboom. Thud! In that moment, the house went eerily quiet. It was the kind of quiet that sent terror up my spine. I hadn't yet heard him climb the stairs to bed as I had so many nights before. I had listened for that often. I knew without a doubt that something horrible had happened. Perhaps my dad died? Why else would the slamming stop?

I gingerly tiptoed to my parent's room. I knew that I would get in trouble for being awake, and for waking my mom. But I didn't know what else to do. I knew I had to tell someone. My dad needed help. Arousing from her sleep-deprived slumber, my mom told me to go back to bed, as she pulled on her bathrobe and trudged downstairs. I listened with hyper vigilant ears for a long time and didn't hear anything. Somehow, with her in charge, I fell back asleep.

The next morning, life seemed to go on as normal that Saturday. Then I saw it — a large black and blue mark right on top of my dad's bare head. I wanted to ask him about it. I wanted to know desperately what had happened. Yet, somehow I knew that I couldn't talk about it — with anyone. I couldn't tell a soul. It had rocked my little world, leaving me feeling drained and alone. And, in spite of everything, my dad was alive!

I didn't know what happened that night or any of the other dozens of nights through my childhood and teenage years when I intuitively felt distress emanating from my dad or mom. As far back as I could remember, I had radar-ears for them. I'd awaken from a deep sleep — terrified. As the fog of sleep cleared, I knew, somehow, that something was terribly wrong in their world. I experienced it deeply in my body, so it also became wrong in my world too. I felt responsible, horribly responsible.

What Is Sensitivity?

I heard often as a child that I was "too sensitive." And the way it was said, it was NOT something that filled me with pride. I heard noises that others didn't hear, noticed things others didn't see, felt things in my body more than others, and worried a lot. I felt anxiety often and didn't know how to calm myself. So I knew sensitivity was definitely a bad trait to have. And I knew I had it.

Perhaps as Doreen Virtue says in *The Sensitive Person's Guide to Clearing and Shielding Your Energy,* "As a highly sensitive person — also known as an *empath* — you feel everyone else's emotions. Your body functions like a vibrational instrument, like a drum vibrating in tune to other people's thoughts and emotions." That's it! I have felt these vibrations all my life.

So I'm an empath! Fifty years later, I am learning that my sensitivity is energetic. I pick up on subtleties. I feel things more deeply. I can see the sadness in someone's eyes even if they don't feel it. I can sense the physical pain in the way a person moves. I can tell the message BEHIND the question that someone asks. I can even feel the distress of someone in another town, if they are deeply connected to me. It's not something I have to work at. It comes to me easily and effortlessly. And now I know how I was able to tune into my dad's distress!

I didn't know what to do with the information I received. Oh, as most kids do, bless their hearts, I probably said things at first, you know, shared my childhood observations and wisdom in a frank sort of way. And it wasn't well received in the early 1960s in a fundamentally Catholic home with strict rules. So I felt odd. Weird. Evil.

"I'm weird. Something is wrong with me!" These affirmations were all I knew for many years. To cope, I'd space out — float above my body — manufacturing a kind of high without a substance and that protected me from absorbing any more information.

"As I thought about the benefits of my sensitivity,
I realized that it had always led me to feel
deeply connected to nature, animals, birds,
music, and art. It had also translated into a
keenly perceptive ability to read people."

~ CHERYL RICHARDSON

So let's fast-forward through my many life experiences and lessons. I kept working on myself alone and with others, like therapists, bio-feedback professionals, wellness coaches, massage therapists, church groups, and more. I grew smarter, more spiritual, and tuned in to myself on a deeper level. I processed many hurts and worked through outdated beliefs. Voila! I finally saw how my body functions like a vibrational instrument to the energies around me.

For example, I love attending cycling races. I cycle myself, so I know how it feels and how difficult it can be. When I attend a bicycle race with hundreds of other enthusiasts, I am excited, energized, and surrounded by many friends. I absolutely love the energy and being outdoors. There is nothing like it.

Incredibly, just as though I'd participated in the race, I can feel totally wiped out the next day. My body fills with adrenaline as if I ran into stress, anger or fear, increasing my heart rate and blood pressure. I feel as if spiders are running through my veins, and I can't sit still. I feel frazzled and overwhelmed, like I had ingested a pot of coffee or a bag of sugar.

And even with the help of meditation and deep breathing, it takes me hours to calm my body and mind, and to feel grounded.

Now, I know. I'm sensitive. As I learn how to protect myself from others' energies, I am embracing my sensitivity. And it can be a good thing. Of course, by deeply connecting to what's around me, I'm careful not to absorb energies I don't want and I do my best to avoid feeling frazzled and on overload.

My sensitivity provides me with valuable information, naturally. It just comes to me without effort. It helps me to be more present, and more mindful. Just as I can fully feel the anxiety and stress, I can also fully experience joy and calm. I can avoid situations more easily that don't feel "right." I can feel how foods, medications and exercise either support or don't support me. The more tuned into myself I am, and what's around me, the better-balanced I am. I am deeply connected to my spirit, my essence, my being. I feel more whole. And it's from this place that I can truly benefit the world and those around me.

 "And being different? That turned out to be the best part of all. I found that, with a little creativity, and a lot of dedication, any difference can be turned into something amazing. Our differences are our superpowers."

~ CECE BELL, EL DEAFO

My sensitivity is my superpower.

What Is A Superpower?

According to the dictionary, a superpower is a power greater in scope or magnitude than that which is considered natural or has existed previously.

"Observe yourself with others or out in nature
and notice what comes very easily and
magically to you. That's your superpower!"

~ DOREEN VIRTUE

I like to look at this energetic sensitivity like the "Fantastic Four." This fictional superhero team appeared in comic books published by Marvel Comics. The story goes that during an outer space test flight in an experimental rocket ship, a storm of cosmic rays bombarded the Fantastic Four. [Source: http://en.wikipedia.org/wiki/Fantastic_Four] Upon crash landing back to Earth, the four astronauts found themselves transformed with bizarre new abilities:

- Mister Fantastic, a scientific genius, can stretch, twist and re-shape his body to inhuman proportions — in any shape he needs. He's the father figure and leader.
- Invisible Girl/Invisible Woman, can bend and manipulate light to render herself, and others, invisible. She later develops the ability to generate force fields, which she uses for a variety of defensive and offensive effects.
- The Human Torch possesses the ability to control fire, allowing him to project fire from his body, as well as generate the power to fly.
- The Thing transforms into a monstrous, craggy humanoid with orange, rock-like skin and super-strength. The Thing is often filled with anger, self-loathing and self-pity over his new existence. Eventually through his trials, he becomes "the most lovable group member: honest, direct and free of pretension."

The four became fantastic, not because they tried to pretend they didn't have "bizarre new abilities." They embrace these abilities, somewhat awkwardly at first, and then decide to use these powers for good as superheroes. It's a "save the world" kind of thing.

Perhaps the Universal Creator gave me energetic sensitivity through a storm of cosmic rays before I arrived on earth. Now that I'm here with my abilities, feeling somewhat awkward at times, I can look at this power as something to understand, embrace, and use for good. Or I can see it as something that renders me bizarre. Like each of the four superheroes in the Fantastic Four, I'm embracing the power I have been given for its true potential, and I'm developing it into an ability that reaches out to help others and the planet.

Accept Your Superpower.

 "The coolly logical part of her brain noted almost sardonically that Edilio had a superpower after all: being Edilio."

~ MICHAIL GRANT

We ALL have superpowers waiting to be loved and nurtured. Yes, even you!

Some sense energies, like I do — we're energetically sensitive. Some talk to souls that have passed on — mediums. Some sense organ overload and distress in humans or animals — medical intuitives. Some predict the future — psychics. Some communicate with animals. As a world, we have just begun to notice our whispers of the heart — so the opportunities are endless.

I now know that I've had this empathic ability since birth, perhaps before. I realize that we are all given amazing abilities that help us navigate through life. I can choose to love and nurture my superpower … which can be fantastic! Or I can choose to keep telling myself that something is wrong with me. It's my choice and my choice alone. So

I'm shifting my thinking. I am seeing this "new-to-my-consciousness" ability as a sixth sense, an unclaimed superpower within me.

Here are some techniques I've learned to embrace and support my superpower of energetic sensitivity.

∾ 1. Tune In

Often, I absorb thoughts and/or feelings — energy, and I don't even see them coming. It can be as simple as having a conversation with someone, that I enjoyed by the way, and I walk away feeling drained, lightheaded or anxious. When my body absorbs too much energy, I feel it.

Mainly, I feel the energy in my heart, the love center, the most — it often skips a beat if the energy hits me hard or suddenly, just like it did when I was seven. I feel it in my stomach as queasy or achy. I can space out (I spent most of my childhood spacey!). Something doesn't feel right.

For now, I'm suspending judgment on the situation, and just noticing. As the words imprinted on a three-year-old girl's t-shirt stated last week, "I am still learning." Yes, I am! In fact, I'd love to have that t-shirt!

So, on most days, I practice kindness and love toward myself, as I ask myself if the energy I'm feeling is mine, or someone else's. Identifying and feeling the physical symptoms allows me to take the next step — ask questions and determine what's happening.

 "There is just no getting around that turning bad things to good things is up to you."

~ DEEPAK CHOPRA

∾ 2. Gather The Power To Fly

When I sense unusual physical symptoms, I ask myself:

    ∾ What am I energetically sensing?

- ↶ Is this MY anger? MY anxiety? MY fatigue? MY frustration? MY embarrassment? Or does it belong to the person next to me? Or the person down the hall? Or someone I love in another area?
- ↶ Did I have any caffeine? Sugar? Medication? Something hard to digest? ... that could be causing this?
- ↶ What are my heart and body telling me?

Once I've done a simple assessment, I use several techniques to return to balance.

↶ 3. Generate Force Fields — Daily

Exercise. For me, this is #1. There is no better balancing technique than moving my body daily to something I enjoy. It may be a fast walk around the neighborhood with the puppies, a hike in the steep hills, a dance class, a hatha yoga session or a bicycle ride. Whatever I choose, it keeps me connected to my body, grounded. It brings oxygen to my cells, clears my mind, and detoxes my body. And it's a heavy hitter. It's mandatory. It works every time.

Get quiet. For me, it's a guided meditation, using my Breathe2Relax phone app, sitting in nature to listen to the birds, or just lounging in my backyard to soak up the quiet the same way I soak up air. Getting enough rest falls into this category too. I've learned, I NEED quietness ... often.

Shield Yourself.

1. I use stones throughout our home that are known to absorb energies, facilitate calm and lighten my energetic load:
   - ↶ Rose quartz — to love and support my heart
   - ↶ Obsidian — to deflect negativity, anger and psychic attacks
   - ↶ Tiger's eye — for protection and strength
   - ↶ Malachite — for absorbing electromagnetic frequencies
2. I ask for the protection of Archangel Michael before I begin my day. *"Archangel Michael, please surround me with protective light that keeps out negativity, stuck and lower energies and psychic attacks. Allow in only love and calm."*

3. I use sage to release all stuck and negative energies. This is a ritual our ancestors used to fill the home with love, and create calm. As I light the sage bundle for the smoke to clear my home, I confirm: *"We lovingly let go of all stuck energies of everyone who enters our home. Our home fills with protective light, and love from corner to corner."*

✧ 4. Love Yourself Completely

The Thing of the Fantastic Four transforms from a monstrous, craggy humanoid often filled with anger, self-hatred and self-pity, to the most lovable one of the bunch — honest, direct and free. The transformation takes time, and work, and is well worth it.

I'm transforming myself too, mostly through accepting myself for who I am.

I am surrounding myself with like-minded people who can nurture, care for, and support me in my sensitivity. As I, in return, do for them in whatever superpower they nurture.

I read books and watch videos from others who have a passion to help us sensitive ones. These mentors embrace their "bizarre new abilities" and become fantastic. They turn fear and doubt into more than bravery. They are on a path to help others transform.

I have a wellness coach who has been instrumental in helping me to recognize my superpower. She works with me on how the energy affects me, and how I can ground and protect myself from taking inappropriate energy inside by body and developing physical symptoms. She gives me many new activities to try to see what works for me. Having a counselor or coach is a must-have.

I am eating pure, whole, organic foods that keep my body grounded and supply it with the best nutrition. I have been tested for mineral deficiencies and know my genetics; I take supplements that are calming and balance my body so that I stay healthy, healed and whole. I listen to how my body feels after a meal to see if it's a supportive food for me.

I find that when I respect my body and its biological and physiological needs, it's so much easier for me to stay grounded and centered.

 "Taking care of my physical body is a
non-verbal affirmation of self love."

~ MIKALA

I look in the mirror and say: "I love you. I completely love you, Michelle." It can be awkward at first, I know. Yet, as I look into my eyes, I am replacing the mantra that something is wrong with me. I am learning what my heart wants me to know. "I am learning" to love myself for who I am for **all** of me, not only part of myself.

 "So how do you love yourself? First of all,
and most important: Cease all criticism of
yourself and others. Accept yourself as you
are. Praise yourself as much as you can."

~ LOUISE HAY

I am learning to "pull the plug" each night to recharge. I let go of the energies around me. Often I have to really work at this — consciously letting go and letting go and letting go again.

You're Invited.

Today, I invite you, along with me, to go within. Sit with yourself. Breathe into your belly button slowly — Exhale. Hear the quiet — drink it in like air. Listen to the birds chirp. Feel the earth under your feet. Feel the wind blow. Eat an organic carrot. Pet your puppy. Cuddle your cat. Look in the mirror and say: "I love you. I completely love you," every time you walk by.

Embrace yourself for all of you, even for those bizarre little-understood abilities that have plagued you your entire life. You know what they are — you were born with them. They come easily to you. So easily, it probably feels downright scary. And you probably don't understand them or think much of them. It is time to do this now.

They are part of the *fantastic you*, the one you were meant to be on this planet, the superpower bestowed upon you before birth.

It's time to tune in to them, listen carefully, and make the most of them. Work out the kinks. Get whatever help or encouragement you need.

They are your spiritual gifts, the whispers of your heart, that you were meant to have the courage to use. Let those superpowers shine through your essence to bring good to the world. Let them bring their good to you. There is nothing that beats the feeling of giving of your self in this way.

You are here to shine your light on the world. Love it and let it shine!

Namaste!

Dedicated to Gordon, Bri and Daria. Thank you for being on my journey with me! And Laureen for being there since your beginning, little sister! And for the lessons I learned with Mom and Dad. Together we are love!

I am grateful to all those brave souls striving to bring knowledge, calm and love to the planet through their superpowers, especially Heather Dane, Louise Hay and the Hay House peeps. I deeply appreciate the organic farmers and food gurus that stay connected to the earth, and tirelessly work to educate us, and to bring us pure, organic, and nutrient-rich foods. Thank you to the food and supplement companies with wholesome missions. And for those helping all animals live in healthy, loving, and safe environments. I am grateful for peace, freedom and the great outdoors. Namaste.

~ Michelle Reese

Kimla Dodds

KIMLA DODDS is a Radio Host and has her degree in Metaphysical Counseling from the University of Sedona AZ. Certified in Astrology, (Western and Chinese) Mediumship, Tarot, Energy Resonance Healing® and is a Feng Shui Practitioner. Psychic from childhood she has worked to accelerate balanced living through counseling services while sharing her acquired knowledge. Her passion and crusade is highlighting the awareness of unseen energy. She is currently residing in Chandler, Arizona and travels the globe teaching, learning and experiencing this wonderful and challenging world called life.

The Visitation

How did I know I was different than all the other kids in my neighborhood? It seemed they included me all the time. After dinner, we all got together and played kick the can or in the summer when the light stayed bright we played baseball until it was late. I was chosen every time to play, even with the boys! I remember laughing with my friends when we compared Barbie dolls and wardrobes. Even chalking out hop scotch and finding the perfect stone was fun with the group and those times became some of my fondest memories. But when I started to talk about things I had discovered like the angels and fairies the atmosphere changed immediately. Every time I mentioned those things my friends said it was time to leave, and quickly gathered up their toys, speeding out on their pink shiny bikes with the handle bar streamers flying in the wind and the clothes pinned playing cards fluttered in harmony.

I couldn't understand what all the fuss was about. Ever since I could remember I would see and hear people in spirit and dance with the wee ones from the fields. I thought everyone could see and hear them. Then in fourth grade President Kennedy was assassinated and I could hear him talking about it while I was silently watching the televised funeral procession. I could also hear loud and clear when Marilyn Monroe herself insisted she was not responsible for her passing. But I loved the special occasions when my Grandpa would come by in the evening and sit at the end of my bed, even though I knew he passed away when I was five. I made my Mom laugh out loud when I told her about the "Martians" outside my bedroom window. She just sighed and said I had quite an active imagination. The entire family looked at me during those early years with a slant to their heads like one side was much too heavy to hold straight. Didn't they hear them as well? Was I the only one?

Happy was the day when I was ten and my mother allowed me to bring home astrology books from the library and work on our birth charts after the supper dishes were done. Elation was the feeling when I checked out books on "How to read palms, faces and body language." However, none of my friends were interested in any of the things I was interested in. When we went to Mass it was an unspoken rule that what I was reading and learning about was somehow taboo. Yes, it was then I realized I was a bit different than the other kids I played with.

Throughout my life I kept hidden my never talked about gifts until my mother and step dad became intrigued with a small farm town called Conyers, Georgia. They retired in Florida and had heard of the Blessed Virgin Mary's visitations to this farm house in close by Georgia once a month. The stories they shared were very similar to the ones I had heard about in another town called Medjugorje in Bosnia. Seemed the Blessed Mother would arrive and speak through an appointed person to translate and give messages to the crowds.

My parents invited me to one of these gathering in an early month of spring. The farm fields of Conyers smelled fresh and fertile. The tiny farm house looked more like a small ranch styled home in a slight "L" shape that had a large lazy front porch with many pillars and rocking chairs. As we waited for the appearance of the Blessed Mother everyone buzzed with excitement. Some shared their photos from other pilgrimages and some were reciting the rosary. I sat in between my folks and focused in on the house itself. It was hard to see the little house as the crowd was swelling and we were feeling the squeeze. Our portable chairs were holding the space and I had a feeling to kneel and begin praying. My Pop looked up in the sky and noticed a huge cross made by white clouds overhead. I closed my eyes and could hear the announcer apologize for the fact that the much awaited time had passed but asked us not to lose faith in her visitation. It was then that the entire crowd started singing the song "Ave Maria." The tone sent shivers up my spine.

That's when I saw something out of the corner of my eye. I looked up to my right in the sky and saw a huge ball of light. Surrounding this light was four other small balls of light and they were traveling very fast. I then had a "knowing", that is all I can describe it as. The "knowing" that the large ball of light was the Blessed Mother and the four other lights were Archangel Michael, Padre Pio, St. Clair and St. Anthony. I could hear my voice announce to my mother that she had arrived and she had in tow, Archangel Michael, Padre Pio, St. Claire and St. Anthony. She said how do you know? I said I saw them coming in. They landed right there in the small farm house. What I found strange was that I had no idea at that time who Padre Pio was and never heard of his name but recited it very clearly. My parents both said that they had been looking and didn't see anything. I wondered, how could I see them and they couldn't? I insisted and that's when the announcement came over the loud speaker translated in four languages that the Blessed Virgin Mother had arrived and accompanying her was Archangel Michael, Padre Pio, St. Claire and St. Anthony. I could still see them, so I closed my eyes because the light was so bright. But even with my eyes closed I could see them all perfectly.

The Blessed Mother was so beautiful and delicate wearing her blue robes and extending her arms. I could not hear her talking but could see her mouth moving along with her hands. She began to cry and seemed terribly upset. The appointed person came forward, a sweet lady with the voice of a five-year-old to translate what her message was. She pleaded with everyone present to honor her son. She stated that even people who were gathered here today would go on to turn their backs on the Lord and not believe or have faith.

At that moment the guilt began to set in. Why could I see her and my devoted parents could not? I certainly was the one that was a sinner from way back according to the Catholic religion anyways. My mom was a regular church goer and raised us in the Catholic faith. My heart felt so heavy that I had to get up and walk away to cry in solitude not to upset the others around us. The burden she carried and tried to convey was so hard to feel and bear. It was crushing, her compassion and intention to reach out to us all. She said over and over again to honor her Son and pray for peace on earth.

Afterward, I came back to sit down and hold the hands of my parents. I expressed my love and gratitude for them. All I felt was the incredible amount of heavenly love and how unworthy I was to be apart of this magical miracle. Then I looked up and saw the same blinding bright lights in the exact formation fly by the crowd and accelerate into the sky. Amazing! Better than any Steven Spielberg movie and I was a part of it!

The announcer then came forward from the expansive porch to validate that she had left and invited the crowd to line up and tour the inside of the little farm house to see the sacred space where the Blessed Mother stood inside the home. I pinpointed the spot from our seats and we moved with the others to get in line. Once inside the modest home there was a statue of the Blessed Virgin Mary right where I had told my mom she was standing. We couldn't even speak — it was too holy a spot to even acknowledge at the time. The image of her crying and pleading kept flooding back to me with such an impact.

We exited the home in silence and knew we had each witnessed a very special miracle. My heart is filled with a passion to proclaim that yes, Mother Mary, the Angels and Saints do exist. Please pray to them and know that they watch over us and will visit us again to provide the proof that some of us need. As I found out, heavenly love overrides the shame and the guilt. You do not need to be perfect to see them or to hear the most High. Humbly I assist others to maintain the balance, harmony and purpose in their lives. I beg of you to pick up your child-hood rosaries, teach others and pray everyday. If you have an interest to learn about the Blessed Mother or how to pray the rosary please reach out. Miracles do happen. I have seen it with my own eyes, open or closed. Share your experiences with others. We are not alone. Love is the message and peace is the goal.

This is dedicated to my earth Mom Margaret, my heavenly Mother Mary and all of my Chinese Masters and World Teachers that have trusted me with their ways of wisdom. In honor and appreciation I bow to all.

My loves, family and friends hold me in an inner circle of light that provides me with strength and a safe place to blossom and grow. I wish to thank them all for their inspiration and support. May a circle of love surround you always.

~ Kimla Dodds

Intuition literally means learning from
within. Most of us were not taught
how to use this sense, but all of us
know that "gut" feeling. Learn to trust
your inner feeling and it will become
stronger. Avoid going against your
better judgement or getting talked
into things that just don't feel right.

~ DOE ZANTAMATA

Renee Essex-Spurrier

RENEE ESSEX-SPURRIER is a Lightworker, Author, Spiritual Life Coach, **Heal Your Life**® teacher and founder of Angelic Creations.

She is trained in many healing modalities such as; Reiki, Aura Soma (Colour Therapy), Tarot and Angel Card Readings, Clairvoyance, Psychic Readings and Healing Breathwork. She also leads numerous workshops and courses on meditation, intuition, how to achieve your dreams, prosperity, soulmates etc. She wrote 'Today's the day I meet my soulmate.' All her work is heart based.

She loves to sing, dance, act, read, write, do yoga, meditate, travel and enjoy many wonderful adventures with her husband and cats. She is romantic, an optimist and believes in miracles. She is also an active animal activist.

She set up her company Angelic Creations as a way to sprinkle more love and light around the planet!

For more information, meditations and FREE Tarot and Angel Oracle Card Readings please go to:

Website: www.angelic-creations.net
YouTube: www.youtube.com/user/angeliccreationstv
Facebook page: www.facebook.com/AngelicCreationsPage

Losing Hope

The story of a little soul's brief visit on earth and the gifts she left behind.

"I can't seem to find a heartbeat." These are seven words that no mother or father-to-be ever wants to hear and, yet, as I lay on the doctor's couch holding back my tears, I heard this and knew that my pregnancy was over.

Miscarriage. No one seems to talk about this subject much. It's a sensitive and awkward topic for most people and, therefore, it is shrouded in secrecy and deemed taboo. Yet what I have discovered from having gone through the experience of losing my baby is that miscarriage is a common occurrence (one in four pregnancies end in miscarriage) — still no one ever really talks about it and couples can go through this painful experience in isolation. A miscarriage represents not only the physical loss of a baby but also the loss of the parents' hopes and dreams, a whole new future that they had allowed themselves to imagine. In one split second, all of that is taken away. A miscarriage is one of the most traumatic and painful experiences any woman can ever go through.

My Story

My husband and I have not had an easy journey with regards to starting a family. It has been full of grief, heartache, longing, frustration, hospital tests and also a nightmarish and failed IVF process. Numerous hospital tests have shown that nothing is medically wrong with either of us, so it has also been a time of great confusion.

When I finally fell pregnant we were overjoyed. And for a few brief weeks we were the happiest we'd ever been in a long time. Only our bliss was to be short lived.

One day I suddenly started spotting blood and experiencing heavy cramping pains. Julian could not come into the hospital with me, as he had to go to work. There was no way he could cancel, as he was the leading man of the show and their first performance was today. It was really difficult for him to leave me and we both cried in the car as he hugged me, feeling helpless. He had no choice but to just drop me off at the car park, watch me hobble into the hospital alone and simply drive away.

Julian was with me the next day though, long enough to witness the beginnings of what I call 'The Fallout.' I was suddenly in excruciating pain as I could feel large amounts of blood pouring out of me constantly, as if a tap had been left on. I sat on the toilet, miscarrying my baby and crying out for my husband "Oh God, why is this happening?…JULIAN!!!!!" Throughout the morning I kept asking Julian to look into the toilet bowl, as I was too afraid of seeing bits of our baby just lying there. Julian valiantly checked each time I went. When I passed a particularly large and painful clot Julian described what he saw to me; a possible broken umbilical cord and a placenta or a sac of some sort. This was horrific and devastating for both of us.

Julian and I would savor the short time we'd have together while he toured the country driving home in between venues whenever he could. I spent my time at home expelling our precious baby from my body. I literally spent weeks on the couch in my robe, clutching a hot water bottle, feeling depressed, but being surrounded by love from my cats, my family and special friends.

One of my friends, Crystal, surprised me by coming to my house to take care of me, later her boyfriend Yo and my mother Sally also joined us. It was a comfort to have them there with me during such a traumatic time. After all I could not be left alone, as I was losing a lot of blood and finding it difficult to walk. It would also be dangerous if I lost consciousness. My mum helped in so many ways, even though she was exhausted, she visited me at home every day and brought me food and medicine and taxied me around. Another beautiful act was that two of my close friends, Irene and Phong, surprised me by showing up at the hospital when I had to have one of my scans. I was so touched by everyone's love and support. I will never forget what they all individually did for me during this time. I am forever grateful.

Julian and I decided to name our baby in order to honour her little life, even though it was but a brief flicker. We named her Hope because that is the miraculous gift that she had given us. She appeared in our lives at a time when we were on the verge of giving up.

Gifts & Synchronicities

Many synchronicities surrounded us at the time, which has led me to believe that my baby's soul had a hand in them.

- ✍ Before Hope I had felt broken both emotionally and physically. After Hope I found a new belief in my body and myself and for the first time I believed that I could actually be a mother in this lifetime.

- ✍ When I had called my friend Irene, initially, and she didn't answer her phone it was because she was singing at a funeral. She said she was staring mesmerized at a stained glass window with the word 'Hope' written on it at the time of my call.

- ✍ On the night my mum drove me to A&E, we had attempted to go to three other hospitals before ending up in the one hospital in the whole country that I adamantly did not want to go to.

Something negative had happened there recently to someone close to me, but due to unavoidable circumstances we ended up there anyway!

∾ On our way to the hospital we got stuck in traffic. I noticed that the car we were stuck behind had a license plate of 444 (the angels' calling card!) If you ever see the number 444 it's your angels' way of telling you they are there, so pay attention. I took it as a sign; it was confirmation that wherever I ended up, the angels would be taking care of me. I was treated very well at the hospital and was told to come back for my scan the next morning.

∾ The interesting thing about this scan was that I had been booked in to go to the first floor of the hospital for my appointment at 11.00 AM the next morning. Unknown to me at the time my sister Rhoda (who I am usually very close to but hadn't spoken to for a year) was also booked in to the same hospital on the same floor at practically the same time (11.10 AM). Our paths were designed to cross! As a result, I finally spoke to my sister and we gained clarity and healing over a previous misunderstanding. A miracle.

∾ Prior to this miscarriage I was also disconnected from the rest of my family for various reasons. My little baby made sure that her brief visit would reunite us and heal us all. Hope intervened and sacrificed her own life to bring us all together. As a result, our relationships are now harmonious and we are healed. What a powerful little soul with such a big life mission. She achieved so much in such a short space of time!

Because of this experience I now believe that:

∾ Souls choose their parents before they are born.
∾ Babies who didn't make it on earth did so by choice.

- ✌ The mother did not do anything wrong, as the baby's soul is equally involved in this choice and process.
- ✌ The mother and father and baby have a three-way soul contract that allows for miscarriages to happen as a way of bringing more clarity, love, wisdom or healing to all parties.
- ✌ Nothing has gone wrong and that everything has actually gone right and according to plan. Everything is always in Divine right order in the universe.
- ✌ There is a higher reason for it all, even if we can't see or understand it.
- ✌ The baby soul might've also had fears and concerns about coming into a human body. Because souls live in the higher realms without the dense and heavy energies of our world, such as fear, pain, anger etc., they might need time to adjust to our much lower vibrations.
- ✌ Souls can elect to have a little test run of their lives on earth by 'dipping their etheric toes in the water' before committing to a whole life here.
- ✌ The baby soul came and went to bring healing to the parents.

So even though we lost Hope, we haven't lost hope. In fact, that's the one lasting gift that she gave us during her brief time here on earth. Indeed the whispers from our hearts tell us to try again. So we will dare to get up and try at least one more time. We must trust God with the deepest faith we can find within ourselves. No matter what the outcome I **surrender** all to Him.

If you are going through this experience, please don't lose hope. Breathe deeply and for now just focus on loving and healing yourself during this traumatic time. Then when you are ready, try to extract the gift from this experience, for there is one there waiting for you even if it is buried deeply in the soil of your consciousness. Mine the gold in the dark. It is waiting to reveal itself to you. There is no one to blame, not even yourself, and the soul that was to become your baby had a life mission and a life plan just as you did before you came to earth. He or she just chose not to incarnate at this time. Earth is a pretty harsh school for souls who live in the light and are used to heaven. I don't blame some souls for having the reluctance to experience an earthly incarnation. So be gentle with yourself and with your baby. I hope my following meditation helps.

Meditation

1. Take three slow deep breaths.
2. See, sense or feel a warm wave of relaxation throughout your body. This warm, golden, Divine light pours down into the top of your head and moves gently down through your face, your neck, your shoulders and arms and hands. This loving energy then pours down into your torso, your chest, your back, your spine and each muscle in your shoulders and back. This healing energy also flows into your belly, your hips and reproductive organs bringing relaxation and healing to these areas particularly as it continues to make its way down into your legs, feet and your toes.
3. Now imagine walking barefoot down 10 warm, wooden steps; 10, 9, 8, 7, 6, 5, 4, 3, 2, 1. Once you reach the bottom you find yourself in a place of natural beauty and feel your feet sink into whatever surface is appropriate for that place (for example; warm sand, grass etc.)
4. As you relax more deeply, letting go of any tension that you may be holding anywhere in your body and mind, now imagine that there is a ball of Light far off in the distance in front of you and that it is coming towards you. What colour is it? This is the soul of your baby. As it comes near, you feel a sense of familiarity, other feelings, thoughts or emotions may also come up. Allow these to come, whatever they may be. Does it look, sound or feel like a female or a male energy, would your baby have been born a girl or a boy?

Stay with your baby's soul for a while and just let this moment be what it needs to be.

5. When you are ready, start to communicate with your baby. You may ask him or her questions or you may simply express how you are feeling. What do you want to say to your baby?

6. Questions that you might like to ask your baby can be: Why did you choose me to be your parent? Why did you leave before incarnating? What was our soul contract or agreement together? What is the gift I can take away from this experience? What gift did this experience give you? What did we learn from this? What can I focus on now, moving forward?

7. Now receive a gift, in whatever form it takes, from your baby (this can be an object, a feeling or a symbol, etc.). Feel free to give your baby angel a gift too.

8. Express your gratitude to your baby's soul and tell him or her that he or she is loved by you (remember that you are loved eternally too!) Now bring this ball of light into your heart (bring your physical hands together onto your heart) knowing and trusting that your baby will always live in your heart and be a part of your life forever more.

9. Then meditate on the word SURRENDER. See it, breathe it, feel it in whatever way it manifests for you today and as you do so, open your hands and arms out to free your baby's soul out into the Universe to go freely where it wants to or needs to be. You can also ask Archangel Michael to accompany your baby for protection and guidance. Trust that s/he is safe with our Maker, our Divine Mother/Father God.

10. And when you feel a letting go, gently bring yourself back, counting up from 1 to 5. Gently move your body, open your eyes and stretch.

Dedicated to Hope — my baby angel and bright shining star. Thank you for your love, your light and your lessons. Thank you for choosing me to be your mother, it has been the highest honour. Until we meet in the kingdom of heaven I will cherish you forever in my heart. This is your story.

 'An angel in the book of life wrote down my baby's birth. Then whispered as she closed the book "too beautiful for earth".'

~ AUTHOR UNKNOWN

I, and my husband Julian Essex-Spurrier, would like to thank the following people, our beautiful family and friends, for helping us through our recent time of darkness;

My mother Sally Montemayor, my father Eddie Montemayor, my sisters Rhoda and Rowena Montemayor, my brother-in-law Michael Hunter, my nephew Ezra Hunter, our friends; Crystal Yu, Yo Santhaveesuk, Irene Alano-Rhodes, Ethan L Phong, Maxine Fone, Rosanne Ainslie, Cristian Valle, Liza Cabrera, Amra Hurley, Polly Dooley and Cris Stovin.

You guys helped us get through this. We appreciate every bit of kindness and support that you each gave us in your own unique, thoughtful and beautiful ways. We love you all.

And thanks to my cats Ginger and Beth-Beth who healed me in their own fluffy ways!

Linda Lee

LINDA LEE is a certified Heal Your Life® workshop teacher and coach who lives in Long Beach, California. She has also worked with a non-profit organization assisting grandparents who have become primary caregivers to their grandchildren. Previously, she worked for 25 years as an award-winning investigative journalist, travel writer and editor. She recently edited a Buddhist book on meditation.

lindalee113@verizon.net

A Still Small Voice

 "I have been a seeker and still am, but I stopped asking the books and the stars. I started listening to the teaching of my soul."

~ HAFIZ

"**I**s everything okay?" he asked softly.

"Yes," I replied. "I just need to think."

I was about ten years old, sitting rigid and still on the living room couch, for a very long time, lost in thought.

"Do you want to go outside and play?" my father asked at various intervals.

"No, I just need to be quiet."

He seemed concerned. I hadn't moved in more than an hour. While I may have looked peaceful and still, my mind was racing, turning over some thought or another, analyzing it from all sides.

It was an excruciating process and it completely absorbed me.

"She's in her own world," I heard my mother say. That was another day. I was gazing out the window, but not in thought. It was as if a beautiful little cloud had surrounded me, the edges blurred, a semblance more than a clear thought. I was feeling and connecting to images, impressions, beauty, and bliss. Moving between the two — thought and intuitive understanding — was always an awkward dance for me, with both asserting to take the lead.

I understood the difference between the intellect and intuition, even when I was young, but was unable to articulate it. What I did know was that the intuitive was blissful and easy, a guided way of knowing and feeling connected to something bigger and greater than myself. But it also seemed too easy, and, God knows, life wasn't meant to be easy.

Although intuition felt right, my rational, bossy mind would convince me otherwise. "You need validation," it would whisper. So I would reach for a book, to anchor my feelings, my inner awareness.

I excelled at academics; achievements were important. In second grade I received a small, red merit pin, emblazoned with a tiny white cross, for being "the best" in the class all year. I've spent much of my life trying to live up to that small pin and what it represented, and in the process, losing, at times, the sense of wonderment that children seem to embrace.

As I accumulated scholarships and was named in honor rolls, I identified more and more with my intellect. My intuitive impressions continued, and I enjoyed them. But somehow I didn't feel entitled to them and kept them secret. I thought of them as fantasies; they didn't win awards.

I was raised in a very strict Catholic German-Irish family, and expressing feelings openly was not encouraged.

When I moved to the Bay Area in California for college, the world became less cerebral to me. I went to symphonies and museums, and watched the Counter Culture unfold. The so-called New Age movement was emerging, and all of this gave me a more intuitive, impressionistic view of life. Art and music were so visceral. I read poetry along with philosophy. I felt more in balance; my intellect suddenly had a counterweight.

My rigid adherence to authority and merit weakened. To be honest, everyone else around me seemed so much smarter and worldly that competition was less essential. It became easier to yield. I was surrounded by others who dreamed and traveled and wondered. It was safe to awaken that part of me again.

After college I longed to study in England, seeking to be surrounded by the beauty that inspired my favorite poets. I explored dance, music, art and theater, along with my course studies.

This is where my real education began, where my intuition came alive. After a year of academic work, I packed a backpack and sleeping bag, and with $600 in my pocket, I traveled as far east as Turkey and Israel, as far south as Morocco, as far north as Scandinavia, and everywhere in between. Sometimes I was with friends, sometimes alone.

With a loose itinerary, I never knew where I would be from one day to the next, where I would sleep, whose company I would keep. But I was deeply satisfied and felt confident and alive. I was content just to "Be." Traveling alone required a constant alertness, openness and trust — not only of others, but in myself. All of my senses were awake, working in harmony.

Sleeping in olive orchards, meadows and the occasional graveyard made it easier to slip into that magical place where the intellect surrenders to intuition … to Spirit. Over a period of three months, I lost all my reference points. Ruins and reality blurred together. Time became meaningless, relationships transitory, and food was never a given. Enjoying a shared cup of coffee could launch me into a blissful state of mindfulness for days!

Once, I remember sitting on a beach in Greece, reflecting that I had no insurance of any kind. At the time, I don't think I recognized that as a metaphor. No insurance, no guarantees. And yet … I could glimpse ancient history and the present at once. I could communicate and understand others without words — a glance, a smile, even giving and receiving a loaf of bread. I was living intuitively with only my inner whispers (and one Eurail map!) as my compass.

Every day I would wonder what the world held for me next, what new adventure was mine to discover. I relied completely on instinct and intuition to guide me. As each day unfolded, I realized that we are all so similar. I saw life as a whole, not in fragments, not in separateness. Countenances of fear, happiness, greed, anger, kindness — they looked the same on everyone.

When I least expected it, an inner truth rose powerfully within me. I slipped inside myself, unaware of others around me packing their morning bags for a new day. "You've been here so long," it whispered. It startled me, made no sense, even though it resonated truth from a very deep place — that my soul had been journeying for a very long time and was seeking to be free.

 "Something is true when it resonates with and expresses your innermost Being, when it is in alignment with your inner purpose."

~ ECKHART TOLLE

After nearly two years, I returned to the United States and was jarred by the sudden need for a self-imposed structure. I felt depressed and cut off from the intuitive trust I'd experienced during my travels. It was disorienting to encounter the world so compartmentalized again, competing for jobs and worrying about the practicalities of a professional life. I began my career as a journalist, and gradually the intellect took over completely — I mistakenly believed that freedom and responsibility could not co-exist. I believed that my travels, and the intuition they brought to bear, were merely a rite of passage. As with all things that are not nurtured or practiced, or when fear is allowed to take hold, something is lost. In my case, I was losing my intuitive connection to Source.

What I didn't know at the time, was that I did not have to give up my intuitive side to still be an accountable human being, having meaningful work and routines. As I embraced my new obligations, I pushed the intuitive further and further into the background. I chose a career that required constant, strong validation, and I became obsessed with chasing information. Inner Truth became less relevant than cold, hard facts. The struggle itself was intoxicating. The harder a story was to obtain, the prouder I was of securing it. Journalism offered *awards* and it was exciting to rack them up. My ego was pulsing at full throttle.

When the intuitive happened to arise, I would often indulge it, sometimes let it guide my life; and things would go smoothly. Then, missing the struggle, I would analyze where this inner knowing came from and question if it could be trusted. Is it imagination, opinion or just a passing thought? Is it silly or informed to take action based on a strong feeling or unreasoned thought? The more I wondered, the more unhappy I became.

Unable to fully integrate my intuitive side and my intellect, it was as if I had split myself in two. I was out of alignment, no longer connected to my deep inner wisdom that whispered truths to me. I had lost the stillness of gazing — out of train windows, into new faces, at a tiny cup of coffee shared by three, and mostly, into myself. Stillness was replaced by restlessness. I no longer had time for it.

Working for 25 years as a journalist, I had listened to and given voice to hundreds of people. The only voice I did not listen to was my own. In my zeal to be objective, I had tuned out that voice.

"When I run after what I think I want, my
days are a furnace of stress and anxiety;
if I sit in my place of patience, what I
need flows to me, and without pain."

~ RUMI

I would think about my days of travel, and it was incomprehensible that it had all been so easy and had required such little work and thought. Why was everything so hard now? What was I missing and how could I get it back?

The answer seemed to lie in indulging too much thought and too much ego. I was afraid to be wrong, to set aside the intellect, to step aside and refrain from judging information that I sensed, felt, heard, or saw when I let go of thought.

All the inner turmoil and analyzing and not trusting resulted in an indefinable sorrow, and many illnesses — and a forced desire for stillness again.

Fast forward many years later: I am sitting with the acclaimed spiritual teacher Shakti Gawain in her living room, trying to explain the difference between my intellect and intuition, still trying to decide which side of me is leading the dance, exhausted by the steps. She asks me to explain where each one would be sitting in the room and to describe each of them.

"Well," the intellect responds quickly, "I would be sitting right here on the left side of the couch. I am in charge. I have lots of books and information at my fingertips — knowledge."

"Ha!" the intuition laughs. "I sit here quietly on the right side, telling you what books to read. Intellect doesn't really know I am charge because I don't need to struggle..."

The competition was over. The dialogue merely clarified and reinforced what I already knew — that the intuitive side was really in control all along. It whispers its strength, and therein lies its power. Its truth will resonate quietly and completely. It won't struggle with you or try to overpower you. That is how you know it is real. It will allow you to yield, and surrender in peace, if you'll only listen.

The bossy intellect still tries to assert itself, but now I am aware of it. I can deeply appreciate all it has revealed to me, how it has helped me navigate life and career, to analyze problems, and give others a voice. In its struggle with the intuitive, it has helped me to grow. I can revel in the moments now where inner awareness resonates quietly and powerfully, without the need to prove itself. I can accept, yield and surrender. Intellect has its place, but no longer rules my life.

Our intuition, our higher self, our inner compass are our invisible centers, which guide us and connect us to Spirit, and act as our bridge to the outer world. Our hearts, our centers, connect us deeply to one another and keep us in balance.

 "Here is my secret. It is very simple. It is only
with the heart that one can see rightly;
what is essential is invisible to the eye."

~ ANTOINE DE SAINT EXUPÉRY

Developing Intuition

 "Within you there is a stillness and
sanctuary to which you can return
at any time and be yourself."

~ HERMAN HESSE

Connect With Breath

One of the quickest ways to get in touch with your intuition is to connect with your breath. This will help you let go of the constant chatter of your thoughts, and take a journey into the stillness within — where the whispers of your inner guidance reside.

You can connect with your breath anytime throughout the day for a few minutes or longer, by just closing your eyes and becoming aware of breathing in and out. Listen to your breath and feel its warmth as you inhale and exhale.

Timeout

When you are facing a challenge in your life, allow yourself a "timeout." Go inside to your sanctuary and sit quietly. The struggle may overwhelm you at first, but just observe it, rather than engage with it. Close your eyes, take a few deep breaths and allow yourself to relax and settle into your body. Allow the quiet whispers to arise and let yourself open to them.

You can place your hand over your heart, which will help you to get out of your head and move into the deepest part of your true self.

Meditation

A daily meditation practice is key to developing your intuitive guidance and learning how to listen. Meditation is a journey through stillness that will help you establish a peaceful inner core. This quiet inner power will help you detach more easily from external pressure and the ego. In this state you can truly find the power in surrendering.

Nature

Spending time in nature is also a powerful way to disconnect from your thoughts and experience the stillness within you.

 "I only went out for a walk and finally concluded to stay out till sundown, for going out, I found, was really going in."

~ JOHN MUIR

This is dedicated to all my fellow pilgrims and seekers, and the unexpected teachers I have met on my journey.

I would like to thank my workshop partner, Heal Your Life® teacher and coach Maggie Cervantes, who is a constant inspiration and a joy to work with. As well, I would like to thank Dr. Patricia Crane and Rick Nichols (fellow poetry lover) for sharing their wealth of love and guidance, and providing a continued safe, supportive environment to lay bare the soul! You have opened a new window on life for me and my students, and I am deeply grateful. "I am safe, it's only change!"

~ Linda Lee

It is through science that
we prove, but through
intuition that we discover.

~ HENRI POINCARE

Deborah Bates

DEBORAH BATES was born and raised in Maine and has spent her life seeking spirit. She is a creator of songs, stories and magic, whether through her writing or her healing clairvoyant work. She brings her life experiences as a lobsterwoman on a small Maine island, a mother of two sons, and her ties to all creatures on this earth into her work as a mystic healer. She resides in the Santa Cruz Mountains, continuing her deep connection to the ocean and its surrounding life.

DebbyBates.com

🌿 Finding Heaven on Earth

I am the human who needs the light, who dances the waves of tall bending grass. I am the woman who delights in the birdsong and soaring wings of raptors flying high. I am the two-legged, who sees the eyes of the wild ones as an opening to the mystery of life, death, and rebirth. I am the elder who takes joy in the wind that roars off the ocean to rustle the trees. I am the one who needs God.

Five years ago I was given a Native American flute to learn to play and to keep for as long as I needed it. I carried my flute out into the field by my home, a golden light space in the midst of the redwood forest surrounding it. As I started playing my prayers to the land, I noticed that the small birds loved listening and would flit back and forth between the trees and sing their own songs to each other and back to me. I took great delight seeing these jays and woodpeckers and flickers, and then, pure joy as the hawks and vultures soared overhead calling out to me. I put down my flute and said, "Hello. You are so beautiful. Thank you for showing yourselves to me. Thank you for the work you do."

As the song of the flute wove in and out, my joy wove in and out of the field creating a space of magic, and the animals started coming out of the woods to greet me, weaving in and out of the field and my life. I listened to the messages from all the creatures, having learned that they are my earthly connection to spirit, having learned to see spirit through my clairvoyant sight and step into the vertical connection to God.

Then one day this past fall, the eagle came. I saw the flash of gold high in the redwood across the field. I sat on the hood of my car, feeling the sun on my body, as he told me his story of this day. I put down my flute and listened.

What is the beautiful song calling me? I have my nest by the sea, but I feel the wave of music pulling me inland. What is the magic that is roaming the field, calling me?

Whoosh. I am here in this tall grandmother redwood watching the woman play her song. Her spirit grows big as the animals draw near. She has opened up to the heart of the land and she sees what is to come.

I see her two cats that she has brought out to the field, so brave, so brave to walk into this hunting ground. She has the senses of my hawk brothers, as she watches her magic cats. They are so innocent, but she is not. She protects them in the field of death, as she lets them live the fullest life they can here on earth. Soon she will bury one right here, deep in the ground among the sacred sage.

The sun stream is hitting my wings and the woman looks up at me, as her eye catches the gold light bouncing off my back. She watches me for hours wanting to see my wings expand in flight. She wants to fly away too, but stays to help the people ground and see spirit, to protect the earth.

The notes in the wind call me back to the time before the people here now, and those who came before. They stir up the time of no people, which we are once again heading toward. Who will wake up and help the Mama earth to die and re-birth herself? Who else hears the sound of the flute in the wind? Who is listening?

The eagle song, spoken so high in the treetops, with the gold from his body spiraling up, takes me to my home in the sky, among the stars and planets, among those who came before, reminding me of my spirit self who gets to go back and forth between worlds. Then, here in the beauty of the field, I get to see the four-leggeds coming out to hunt and rest. I remember the bobcat who comes through every few months, walking down the driveway and sitting by the shed, looking at me and not moving, telling me with his eyes that this is his field, his mating and hunting ground. I am just a visitor, and if I respect his home, I can stay.

I remember the coyotes yipping in the night reminding me to hold my cats close to home, and the day I went out to the edge of the field to lay down in the sun on my chaise lounge and saw the huge, muddy paw prints of a mountain lion, his fur matted in the cushion. That day, I did not lie down. I shivered as I realized he had taken refuge there. I was stunned that I shared a chair with a lion.

One morning I looked out the French doors of my cabin and saw that my golden cat Thomas had jumped the gate and was out in the field of wet grass hunting for gophers. His hind legs were so stiff from arthritis that he looked like a drunken sailor walking. His back was turned away from two deer that slowly approached him, eating their way across the dewy grass. I held my breath as I saw the larger deer getting nearer and nearer to Thomas, who now sat still, slowly glancing over his shoulder to check what was happening.

Meanwhile Tom's brother, Huckleberry, was just inside the closed gate, peeking around through the wire fencing. He kept looking back at me as if saying, *Oh my God, Mom, do something. Look how big they are. Mom, you need to go save him.* As Huck kept up his vigil, the larger deer reached Thomas and gently put her nose down to his back, sniffing him over and over again. Thomas sat so still and tall. He looked like an Egyptian sphinx. Huckleberry bolted through the cat door into the cabin, no doubt to hide his head under his paws waiting to see if his brother would ever come back.

I let the scene unfold as the second deer moved closer. I knew that deer do not eat cats. I trusted that this was an experience that we were all supposed to have and that I just needed to be ready for when Thomas had had enough. And then he silently called to me — that moment was here. I left the porch and quietly opened the gate as Thomas slowly moved away from the deer, stately as a king, and returned to me.

"Wow, Thomas, you are so brave. That was quite a healing you got." I let him hear my voice as I held a safe path for him to return home.

Later I sat on the couch with Thomas, as Huckleberry sprawled on the rug by the woodstove. As we sat there quietly in meditation, I felt the gentle energy from the deer radiate out to wrap itself around us, filling our home with love and compassion. I closed my eyes and felt the connection between all of us, the animals, the birds, the trees, the sacred sage and the humans. We are never alone or apart in this world. We watch some step up and be brave. We watch others stand behind gaining courage. We watch those who fly above and see the big picture, and those who hold space like the trees and let everyone walk in safety, or not, to take our next steps.

My heart kept opening as I realized that we are all walking in the eternal flame of God. There is no need to be afraid, to worry about death or to protect any of God's creatures from experiences that they have come down here to live. I saw how only I step in the way of God's love for me and remembered we are all eternal souls. I knew that Thomas had brought this reminder to me from the deer. But at that time, I did not know why.

One month later we had to let go of Huckleberry. He died in my arms, purring as he crossed over to the Rainbow Bridge where he got to be free from the pain of his body. He is buried out in the field, just as the eagle had foreseen a few months before, a stone angel marking his space in the world he loved.

The journey I have taken to get to this spiritual life has not been an easy one. I have had to learn to step into my body. Then after years of practicing that with my clairvoyant work, I needed to learn how to step out of my body, so that I could allow spirits who have passed over to come down and communicate through me to those left behind. This whole process of waking up to spirit has been a journey that started when I got clean and sober at thirty-one. Twenty years later I found my spiritual teachers who taught me to meditate and run earth and cosmic energy through my body, waking up my whole self, and stepping into my clairvoyance, seeing life from my third eye and crown.

Watching the animals and hearing them talk to me has been the connection that opened my heart. In this field above the Pacific Ocean I have finally connected my earth self, to my higher self, and thus feel my connection to God. Aligning vertically up to God has changed my life. I no longer fear death. I know that all is one; life and death, animals and humans, trees and sky. There is no separation and, in finding my heart, I get to have all the colors for myself that I thought were bright just for others.

I sometimes cry because blue is so crystal, and green so life-filling rich. Yellow is the joy in my heart and pink the tender love of myself. Purple will take me across to the other side and orange and red fill me with the deep, wild lust for life. These colors flow through me when I go to teach others to be here, present, in the full richness of life that is connected to all. We are constantly moving through life's lessons and the animals that wander this field outside my door, continue to show me life in present time with limitless love, compassion and connection to all that is.

Dedicated to my sons, Owen and Keith Willis — you guys rock. I love how you continue to amaze me.

I have much gratitude for my spiritual teachers: Kris Cahill, Ken Jones, Lisa French, Michael Tamura and Cody Edner. I also want to thank my peers, Suzanne Schiller, Amiel Landor, Nathan Riding, Monica Pappe and Hi'ilani Lynch. Great love out to my fellow animal diviner, Aarin Wood. Gratitude to Vanya Erickson and Laurie Mikulasek. Also thanks to those who help me live one day at a time.

~ Deborah Bates

A hunch is creativity trying
to tell you something.

~ FRANK CAPRA

Brenda Fedorchuk

BRENDA FEDORCHUK is an author, a Life Coach and a Workshop Leader. As a Licensed and Certified **Heal Your Life**® Teacher and Life Coach, Brenda teaches simple yet transformational techniques based on the principles and philosophies of Louise Hay.

Heart Centered Solutions was founded by Brenda out of her desire to follow her true passion and life's purpose of creating a safe space for personal growth. Brenda empowers people to develop a greater sense of personal power, inner wisdom through self-love and compassion so that they can create a life they desire filled with more joy, passion, prosperity and health.

www.BrendaFedorchuk.com
www.heartcenteredsolutions.ca
www.facebook.com/HeartCenteredSolutions

❧ I Am Enough!

I am Safe! All is Well! I am Enough! I must have written these three affirmations down a dozen times in my journal that night. Over and over again I wrote them hoping that this time the universe would respond and magically transform my life so I'd never have to endure pain, suffering or challenges again. How did I find myself in this dilemma? Why did this happen to me? What was wrong with me? What was this all about? What lesson did I need to learn?

I believed that if I did my affirmations and thought positively, I would never again slip into the dark shadow side of self-doubt and unloving thoughts. As my tears fell slowly and gently on the page, they blurred the words I wrote. I surrendered and prayed for a Miracle.

THE COLLAPSE

"You are to sit at your desk and get the work out and nothing else. Do you understand? I am the Manager here, just me and not you! As for those ideas and suggestions you had about leadership and working together as a team ... well ... how do you possibly think you could implement them? Look at you ... all dressed up and looking so put together! Every day when you come in here dressed like this, do you not realize that you are intimidating your co-workers?"

This was my very first face-to-face meeting with my new boss. I came with an open heart ready to share the ideas she had asked me to bring to our meeting. Ideas on leadership, teamwork and what I needed to be successful in this unit. I was thrilled to be asked. I had been looking forward to this meeting. I had experience with some leadership tools that really worked and I was eager to share. I wanted to create a good working relationship. I had heard good things about this manager, like our similar interests in leadership and personal development and how we had been both been trained in a unique leadership discipline.

After getting alone behind closed doors with her, I soon learned that her leadership style and mine were not at all a match. What I encountered was marginalization and not leadership. This was the first of many meetings and situations where she took liberties to publicly embarrass me, especially at team meetings, purposely set me up for failure by providing me with inadequate information, and withheld the training I needed for this job. She made several attempts to ruin my reputation by spreading rumours and attempting to carry out an assassination of my character behind my back. Unfortunately, the things that happened were very subtle and difficult to prove. She smiled through all of it, making little jokes about it. I knew enough to pay attention to how my body was reacting, and my body told me that this was very real and I WAS in danger.

All the work I had done on myself to heal from the difficulties in my childhood and create my best self were at risk. The old messages of not being good enough began to creep back in. Each time another incident happened at work, I would emotionally collapse at home, feeling like a five-year-old child without any protection, personal power, safety or hope that things were going to improve. I felt trapped.

Each day I came to work feeling a whole range of emotions. I seemed to move between feeling angry, ashamed, humiliated, embarrassed, and an added deep sense of isolation generated by being in this predicament. I felt responsible to fix it — but no matter what I did, I could not improve my impasse. I could sense that people at work, outside my unit, had heard the stories. They were moving away from me, limiting their contact with me, because in this workplace it was a career-limiting move to associate with someone management had deemed unworthy and they instinctively knew you had to protect yourself.

By putting pressure on myself to keep up appearances, seem confident, be strong, stand up for myself and not let it bother me, I was determined to just kept soldiering on. I lived in fear that I would be criticized for being too sensitive if my true deep wounds were revealed. I ignored the signals my body was sending — the headaches, the backaches, the sore neck — and kept telling myself that I could handle this. Frankly, truth be told, I had successfully managed much worse in my life. Nevertheless, living in this constant state of total toxicity and dysfunction at work eventually took its toll and I was brought down to my knees.

What I Discovered While On My Knees

 "The only thing necessary for evil to triumph is for good men to do nothing"

~ EDMUND BURKE

I knew I had to do something, but what? My self-esteem and confidence were at an all-time low. There was now a thick steel wall built around my heart … nothing was getting in to hurt me anymore! I felt I was losing my connection to my inner wisdom as fear had taken over, and trusting myself became more and more difficult. I prided myself on being a hard worker. I would work harder and harder, often to my personal detriment, to try to convince others of my worth and value. Nothing I did seem to matter. The position I found myself in seemed completely impossible to navigate. Holding this pain and resentment occupied a good deal of space in my mind and body, in a very negative way. I was beginning to see the effects on me both physically and emotionally. Was

I really doomed to live this life of misery, focusing on drama without much happiness?

I prayed many nights for a miracle. The definition of a miracle that I am referring to is in accordance with the definition used in "The Course in Miracles," which says that a miracle is a shift in perception — the ability to move from, "I Can't" to "How Can I?"

Late one night in the silence, I sat alone journaling when I received a message. A crucial message that I had perhaps once known, but not heard for some time. It was a gentle, loving whisper coming from my inner wisdom, from my heart where a tiny crack in the steel walls had opened. My logical mind did not seem to want to comprehend.

"You are Enough! Brenda, you are enough! You are loved more than you know. This is not about what she or others believe about you. What do you believe about you?" Suddenly, I remembered a quote I knew from Louise Hay's teachings:

 "No person, no place, and no thing has any power over us, for 'we' are the only thinkers in our mind. When we create peace and harmony and balance in our minds, we will find it in our lives."

~ LOUISE HAY

I had been giving all my power away to the authority figure in my life — my boss. This was not the first time, I had done that in my childhood home, as a child as well. I often trusted people who should not have been trusted, who did not have my best interests at heart. I thought it was the thing to do. They were in charge, did they not know best?

At that point, I changed this personal power drain by learning to set new physical and emotional boundaries: I have the right to follow my own core values and standards; I am the only authority figure in my life; what I think and believe is right for me. No one else could know this but me!

As time went on I worked on forgiving myself, and my boss, in order to release my mind from the constant spin cycle of living in a fearful constricted state.

I now see that this crisis was actually a blessing. It put my life once again into perspective and taught me what was truly important: to love my family and friends and use the time I have left on this earth wisely. No one on their deathbed ever said, "Gee, I wish I had done more work!"

Progress Not Perfection

Each day I stay curious for opportunities to learn more about how to be the best me I can be. I take time to love myself more every day. I let go of the judgement and embrace the days that I find myself in the messiness of life when I have momentarily stepped away from my centre. Those days are becoming fewer and farther between but they still do happen from time to time.

I gave up the need to be perfect. I simply do my best each day and know that wholeheartedly expended effort is enough … because when I show up with all my gifts and talents, I am truly enough.

I follow my daily practice and sprinkle it with humor. Humor tends to remind me not to take myself so seriously. I remember that as a human being I will be a work in progress until the day I take my last breath. I trust in my ability to regain my balance and create a space where I can operate from my highest good.

 "Our greatest glory is not in never falling,
but in rising every time we fall."

~ CONFUCIUS

I regularly check in with the wise sage wisdom of my heart. I notice when my thoughts are negative and replace them with uplifting ones. I notice when I am working only from my intellect (inside my head). I stop and drop into my heart, so I can connect with my inner wisdom. I put my hand over my heart and ask, "What is it you need me to know?"

I thought because I said daily affirmations that I would have an easy life all the time. I beat myself up over it thinking that somehow I was doing something wrong, not being good enough. But, the reality is everyone has challenges and drama in their life, no one has a life without burdens. Now, I regularly use this affirmation:

"Life's Lessons come to me easily and effortlessly!"

When I Feel Stuck

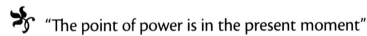 "The point of power is in the present moment"

~ LOUISE HAY

Whenever I feel stuck, I remind myself that it is only a thought and a thought can be changed. I ask for a miracle, a shift in perception. I pray to help me see this situation differently. I am human and, as long as I am on this earth, I will periodically face challenges and perhaps a bit of drama. That experience does not make me a bad person and it does not mean that I have failed to keep my commitment to myself to show up as my highest good and share my gifts and talents in the service for others. In fact, it is the opposite, it is just life and no one, no matter how perfect other's lives may seem, walks through life without challenges and a bit of drama. No one!

I make a conscious decision to choose the best thoughts and behavior that I can in the moment. When I do not know what to do, I do nothing until I check in with my heart's wisdom.

I'd like to share with you three of the questions I use when I am stuck that help me propel forward:

1. Do I have time to stay stuck in my story?
2. Do I have time to live worrying about what others think of me?
3. Do I have time to spend on things that no longer serve my highest good?

I forgive myself for finding myself stuck. I let go of all criticism. I know that criticizing and beating myself up no longer serves me and can shut down the very thing that I am trying to create — living with an open loving heart and finding continuous growth through positive movement. People only change when they feel safe and I created a safe space for change by learning to love myself more.

Daily Practice For Loving Myself More

 "If beating yourself up worked, you'd be thin, rich, and happy. Try loving yourself instead."

~ CHERYL RICHARDSON

1. Repeat often! "I am ENOUGH"
2. Stop scaring myself with fearful thoughts, replace with kind gentle thoughts.
3. Be grateful. Find five things a day to be grateful for and write them down.
4. Breathe. Stay present and be in the moment
5. Make friends with the mirror. Look in my eyes in the mirror and say, "I love you! I really love you"
6. Trust that I am divinely guided
7. Find ways to feel good about myself. Take a bath. Read a good book. Get a massage. Talk to a trusted friend.

8. Protect my energy by only surrounding myself with people who support and love me and by giving myself permission to limit the time I spend with others who drain my energy.

Things I Know For Sure

I believe in miracles, a shift in perception is available to each of us, we just have to ask to see things differently. I have no doubt that I have all the answers I need inside of me. When I am connected and listen to the wisdom of my heart, I lovingly have the power to choose thoughts that support my desire to live a life full of happiness, peace, joy and laughter, while sharing it surrounded by like-minded people.

I also know that my personal history has prepared me to have complete confidence in others' ability to walk over that bridge from self-doubt and suffering, to create their best life through the connection, guidance and wisdom of their heart center.

I know that I needed to gently and lovingly polish off the darkness that temporarily surrounded my heart, and once served to protect me, to allow the brilliance of my inner golden light of wisdom to beam out from my heart. When I embrace my inner wisdom that exists there within my heart, I know that I am safe — no matter what is happening in the world around me.

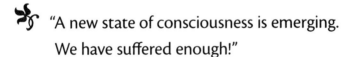 "A new state of consciousness is emerging.
We have suffered enough!"

~ ECKHART TOLLE

I am Enough! I am Safe! All is Well!

I would like to dedicate this book to all the people who have ever felt marginalized and bullied in their life …

Sending thanks to my husband, Pat, and my two amazing children, Amanda and Jeremy. Your unconditional love, unwavering faith and support has created the space that allows me to pursue my dreams. You each have amazing gifts and talents to share with the world. I love you always and forever!

~ Brenda Fedorchuk

Katina Gillespie

KATINA GILLESPIE is a Certified Peace Love Wings®, Mind Body Spirit Practitioner and Workshop Facilitator, an active volunteer with A Cause 4 Paws dog rescue, and an office administrator. She was raised on a farm in Charleston, Illinois and now resides in Orlando, Florida with her cat, Karma and dog, Kiwi.

Her passion is to encourage people to develop and move onward and upward in their lives. She has a Bachelor of Science in Psychology, Masters in Restaurant/Hotel management, and a PhD in the school of Life, as it has brought her to this perfect place. It's as good as it gets!

KatinaEHW@gmail.com
Emotionalharmonywellness.com

❦ Angel Box Diaries

I was living the dream like anyone else in their 20s; college degree … check, married … check, moved into a new city … check, a restaurant manager … check, and my husband was working toward his culinary education. We had amazing plans to open a restaurant of our own, buy a house, and build a future. I was on the "river of life" racing in my "life boat" forging ahead into greatness.

My naïve desire to succeed was certainly taken advantage of by my new employer; it involved working crazy mad hours with a 12-16 hour workday plus taking home spreadsheets, ordering and schedules! I was bar manager so the orders had to get in at certain days and times during the week in order to get timely delivery to ensure customer satisfaction. God forbid, the customer was ever left wanting! To sum it all up, I normally only took one day off a week and a short day was ten hours. A year into my tenure at my first manager position, I was at work and my left side went numb, my speech was slurred and vision blurred. What do I do now? This was not the first time this happened but it was the first time while I was at work. My brother moved down from Chicago after I spent time in the hospital from a previous episode. Of course, my husband was unavailable, but I was able to contact my brother. He rushed to the restaurant like "Speedy Gonzalez" and drove me to the emergency room. To this day, I have no idea how we got there safely! The medical staff went through their checklist and checked my heart, brain scans, monitored my vitals. It was decided to admit me into the hospital after six or so hours in the ER. My brother was my lifeline and stayed with me until he knew I was being admitted. He was there through the white rapids. My husband visited for a few moments to bring me a teddy bear before he was off to his next culinary adventure. The doctors believed that I had a minor stroke or a TIA. They recommended that I see a neurologist and a hematologist. I followed all the doctors' orders. I started taking Coumadin; exercising, and upgraded my diet. When I saw the hematologist we discovered a blood disorder that would prevent me from having children. The doctor advised a hysterectomy due to the complications of pregnancy. My husband did not like to think that I was injured or needed to be fixed. He wanted to believe that I was perfect and so did I. So we both pretended it wasn't there and went on with our lives. I decided that I did not want to make such a permanent choice, so I did not have the procedure.

I had returned to work a day after I was released from the hospital to come back to the increasing demands! I was assigned the entire front of the house schedules (bar, servers, bussers, food runners, and hosts). I was also responsible for training all of them as well as managing the bar. A few months after my return the general manager sat me down and told me he was letting me go due to performance issues. The fact is that I was considered a liability since I had health issues. They purposely assigned me too many tasks so that I would be unable to juggle all of them. I didn't realize this when it was happening, so I turned in my keys and left to self-medicate at the expense of my liver, with my tail between my legs believing that I was a failure.

After a couple of weeks, I was hired on as a server at a new restaurant. Who would think that I would meet my earthly spiritual guides in such an unexpected place? The opening team met in a hotel banquet room for our opening ceremony. I still remember the songs played during the introductions of the corporate team. The energy was electric! I knew that it would be something wonderful! At first I was disappointed that they did not have any management positions available and I was hired as a server. I felt degraded, but at the same time did not feel worthy of management after failing my first attempt. Through the course of training we all got to know one another, sharing our biographies and having adult beverages after work. Many of us came from management background. I became close to two particular individuals that I spent time with, in and outside of work. One sang Karaoke and sounded JUST like Barry White!!! Other servers and I had so much fun being his groupies at the bar. The other was a woman of many talents who moved up from Miami with her man so that they could escape some stresses and write. We all had our unique stories and I found both of them to be spiritually guided, as we peeled away the layers. I was a sponge for their information, absorbing every word they spoke. It was without judgment, encouraging and free of fear. This was a new world compared to my organized-Christian religious background. They did not pressure their beliefs or try to convince me of following any path or rules. The only rules were unconditional love, understanding and acceptance. One is a Shaman and energy worker, the other a Celestial Being who is a messenger of sorts. I was somewhat a sceptic to all of it — listening with interest but reluctant to believe due to the outside influences of my upbringing. It was an amazing chapter in my journey.

I left that restaurant to open a fine dining Italian restaurant as a manager where I wrote the employee handbook, trained the opening team, and planned the extravagant opening! There were celebrities that frequented the establishment. The food and atmosphere were incredible and everyone wanted to be a part of this team. We had an amazing New Year's Eve party. However, I quickly noticed after opening that there was no food cost, liquor cost, or labor cost. My purpose was to unlock the facility and be "tits and a smile". This restaurant was literally owned by a garbage guy from Jersey!!! I was LIVING on the set of The Sopranos!!! The Capone brothers would come in for lunch and we were only open for dinner. The chef would stop his prep work to discuss what they were having for lunch. Then I would pair a nice wine with whatever they ordered or make them mixed drinks. Whatever they desired!

My husband and I were both dedicated to our jobs and our lives rarely included one another. I felt his jealousy of my success. I was working in HIS dream restaurant. I was his trophy that he would take out once a week when we had a day off together. The fact is that we were not in love anymore. We were going through the motions, coasting on our lifeboat and going nowhere. I worked 80-hour weeks so that I did not have to feel emotion.

I wanted to learn more about this amazing spiritual world that I was introduced to and make an impact on our global future. He wanted big houses, fast cars, expensive clothes, and fame. My Shaman and Celestial Being remained in contact. Life happened, and we all went down different rivers. Some periods of time were longer than I ever wanted, and I feared that I had lost them forever, but they truly never left my thoughts. They were always in my lifeboat or at least checking the tide and throwing me a lifeline. They were there to advise when things got tough in my marriage and gave me options and views of thinking that I would have never considered. They never told me what to do. Any changes that happened were going to be MY choice and mine alone. My brother who was living with us did the same. I had a trifecta of positive influence in my school of life.

After unfaithfulness, disrespect and heartache, I took a leap of faith with my newfound confidence to dissolve the marriage. Of course, letting go of the marriage was another failure in my book of torment; another dead end stream where I had to paddle my way out. This found me in a whole new world of darkness, even though I was surrounded by light. I had grown so accustomed to being told that I was not good enough, or pretty enough, or smart enough that I believed it and continued to say these things to myself. I had been advised by my Celestial Being to take three things that I was having difficulty with and to write them down on a piece of paper in a positive way (I am strong,

I am self-confident, I am balanced), surround them with white light, tuck them away and revisit them in a month. I did, but continued to have difficulty with them for the longest time. I never forgot about this exercise, but initially it did very little to improve the areas.

Through my divorce I continued to work at this outwardly-fabulous place and put on my stage face. However, things at work were getting worse, as far as living on the set of The Sopranos. It was obvious I had to leave in order to keep my integrity intact. Something in my soul told me to get out! I was not comfortable there. I gave them a month notice, parted ways and moved on to another restaurant opportunity that promised smoother waters. I was transferred out of state to a location for a temporary assignment. Arrangements were made for me to stay in an extended-stay for an unknown amount of time.

After a month, I was told that I was going to be staying in that city and I was to find an apartment as soon as possible! Mentally I was not in a good place, since I was in a new city, recently divorced, knew no one, and working six days a week!!! Somehow I was able to find the perfect place and made arrangements to have my furniture delivered shortly after I signed the lease. It was all working out! I remember speaking with my dad shortly after I moved into my new apartment. Out of nowhere he says to me, "I know why they call you Kat!" I'm thinking to myself. "Dad, I don't need a lecture," but I entertained him and said, "Why Dad?" He said "Because no matter what life hands you, you always land on your feet! And this time is not going to be any different!" It was exactly what I needed to hear! He had divine timing! I've had a knack of keeping my family guessing in my journey. They never know which turn I will take next or from where I will be calling. Nonetheless, they love me all the same.

I ended up in the hospital again after I had switched to yet another restaurant. I had the same symptoms as before, after working 28 days straight with the shortest one being 10 hours. This time I got a spinal tap, as they feared that I had meningitis, multiple sclerosis, or another auto-immune disorder. Thankfully all the tests came back negative! As suggested by my neurologist, I decided to make a career change. I became an assistant general manager at a hotel and quickly took over the general manager position! I was only working 50 hours a week and felt like I was on vacation! Within a year of working there, the management company decided not to renew their contract at the property. I discovered that the GM is the first to go when new management takes over, so I assisted in the transition and made arrangements to manage another property within my management company's portfolio down in Florida. However, there was a TOTAL breakdown in communication and the property had no clue about me when I arrived! Amazingly, this worked out for the best because I was hired onto an opening team for a worldwide hotel company. I worked for the company for almost four years and with hard work and dedication was promoted three times to move up the ladder quickly.

This is a very quick synopsis of my life of taking leaps of faith without a guide on unfamiliar waters! I did my best to spread my wings and soar, only to find that there were always people there to pluck those feathers so that I couldn't fly straight or as high as expected. There were many frightening moments, many moments I felt I was drowning. I fell out of my life boat. I made mistake after mistake, which catapulted me in the exact direction I was meant to go. I don't regret any of it, because all of the wrong choices led me to the right place.

I remember being consumed with guilt for I was living the dream of others and I felt no joy. I have a graveyard of nametags and business cards that mean nothing to me other than notches in my mantel.

However, over the past few years, I've learned that my external circumstance is insignificant if my internal circumstance is broken, lost and void of aspirations. If I have no purpose, my surroundings will feel purposeless too. I felt like a bird that had all of its feathers plucked and I was lying helpless on the sidewalk unable to move. I found myself self-medicating with alcohol, drugs, and sex; whatever was easiest and available at the time. I was soul-searching with all the wrong tools. I was not looking inward. I looked to see what others were doing. How could I please and not disappoint those around me? I felt empty and unfulfilled and wanted more. After my divorce I was in a seven-year relationship that dissolved two years too late and I felt helpless. I had soared high and travelled further than I ever imagined. I didn't have any goals, so I didn't know where I was going. Every time I moved jobs, cities, and men, I attempted to follow my voice within, without much success. It wasn't until I silenced my world that I found my voice. I had it all along, but didn't recognize it. I was giving myself freely — spiritually, emotionally, physically, and doing nothing to re-charge ME.

Throughout my journey I have done my best to call on angels and my guides here on earth to speak with them occasionally, but it was rarely about how I was feeling; instead it was just to update daily happenings and successes. They gave me tools and trinkets to assist me in finding my purpose. I did not realize that was what they were doing and maybe they didn't either, until I found it — I found my purpose. I was jumping from jobs, cities, relationships all to create what? What was I doing it all for? Behind the name tags, leadership, and training classes was a very weak and lost person. In a world where we are bombarded with dreadful images and angry words, we are constantly seeking hope, something that is full of light. I needed a beacon of light that could light the sky and pave a path.

Then I realized that I had been going through the dark so that others can see that light. **I am the light!**

All these years I've learned to place life decisions and questions up in my Angel Box. The angels and universe will decide what happens and how it will fall. It may not be the answer I am looking for or in the time frame that I am expecting, but the answer will come. I've learned to embrace it, dance with it, sing along and know that it is my purpose! I listen to my inner guides regardless of what others may say. This means that I look inward to find my strength, confidence and balance. The people around me inspire, love and encourage me in my lifeboat, but my angels take the wheel. As long as I listen to my heart, it will guide me to the perfect place.

Dedicated to all the people, places and things that have been with me through the tides, turns, white rapids, floods, trickles, and calm waters in the River of Life! Because of you … I know and love myself more freely.

I am filled with gratitude for my earth angels, spiritual guides, and mentors that have influenced and continue to influence me along my journey. I wish a special thank you to Matthew, Julie, and Roland for your continued inspiration and knowledge. To my parents whose unwavering love and support has provided me boundless freedom, my gratitude and appreciation are endless. And to Lisa — thank you for this amazing opportunity to share my story. Namaste!

~ Katina Gillespie

Catherine Madeira

CATHERINE MADEIRA is a freelance writer and artist. She has been receiving ethereal information for years and is now sharing it in the hope of helping others in their life journeys.

Catherine is from the Reno / Tahoe area with her two children — Jason, who has always demanded an intellectual approach to life, and daughter, Kendal who was born a very old soul. Catherine has been a supportive, open-minded mother who allowed her eccentricities to expand. Subsequently, she has been able to receive, evaluate, and compile the information to pass it along to others.

Umbriel03@gmail.com

Premonitions of
an Empath

Awareness of all of the wonders that this world has to offer is important to our evolution and empowerment on Earth. Therefore, I would like to share with you one category of my experiences pertaining to PREMONITION — and how it feels to bear the weight of being an EMPATH.

My life and behaviors are governed and controlled through the filters of a hypersensitive Empath. I am profoundly affected by the nature of what happens on this planet, including everything from the mobile, living creatures to the plant life, right on through to the planet herself. I cannot be around groups of people, as their energy bombards me with too many opposing moods and kinetics, it leads to dizziness, physical and visual distortion and causes problems with my balance. Having this degree of absorption has driven me to be very introverted, as to avoid input overload. The introversion then leads to a great deal of thought, contemplation, and analytical examination of absolutely everything I encounter. I am a Vegan, and even that makes me feel censurable because plants are also among the living and, if given the choice, I wonder if they would probably rather I not eat them.

I bring up the Empathic factor because these specific premonitions that we are discussing all have a direct connection to single individuals, and are of a very significant and sensitive nature, however, they are true so I have chosen to share them with you.

My premonitory experiences can have a dramatic range — presentation, level of clarity and so on. No two approaching events are the same, so logically each viewing experience is going to vary in the same way.

I have stood as witness to premonitions that were so clear in every detail, that upon exiting the experience it took a moment to realize that it had not yet happened. To clarify, I do not just see a place. I see the total unchanging surroundings, time of day or night, weather temperature, cloud formations, air humidity, scents, sounds, and also complete physical sensory feelings, responses to peril, fear, and terror, or to humor, laughter, elation, etcetera. In several cases, the seeming reality of my presence in this place required my urgent need to immediately evacuate the experience. These premonitions, to my knowledge, seem to be set in stone and they appear to happen in the exact way they were previously seen, unless the WILL of a single person is enough to alter an approaching event. However, let's get further into this possibility at another time.

In the case of the true premonition, some excruciatingly frustrating obstacles present themselves:

1. I generally drop into the occurrence only moments before the incident begins.
2. Though I have totally clear input, I can't distinguish the location. The only way is to recognize the terrain and such, then a general region can be estimated.
3. I have no way of knowing the exact date of an incident, since my purpose there is to be a witness, not to change things.
4. Usually, the incident runs its course, in the world's reality, two days to two weeks after the vision … but this can also vary. In a moment, I will share a precognition that still has not to come to pass.

5. What follows are three examples of near future and far sight. These examples also explain one of the roles I play in these experiences as an Empath.

First Experience

In 1994, I made the grave mistake of not trusting my inner "whispers" and premonitions, my reasoning being that it didn't seem possible to me that this could happen. I was totally confused and befuddled by what I knew as premonition, because such a thing was very unlikely and because of the simple odds against it. But even with my self-denial it came to pass just as I had seen it — 48 hours following the vision and my direct interaction in it.

The premonition opens and I am outside during the daytime and it is very hot. I am on a steep hillside and in the company of what seemed to be about 15 people. Some were wearing long khaki pants and others were wearing blue jeans. They were also wearing boots, while some had on hard hats, and their faces were dirty. Each man was carrying equipment, shovels and other things, and then I realized they were firefighters. The terrain was rough with shrubs, bushes and some trees. I could smell the shrubs, and I knew it was very dry. The dust was rising up as the men moved along and I could smell it and I felt dust going up my nose. I could also smell the smoke. The mood of the men was fast, we were all moving fast. Now I'm among them. I was moving as quickly as I could and I was following someone. There was an urgency combined with a mix of fear, control, fast flight, and a determined focus on escape — at all cost.

I was getting a grasp on the situation. The men were fleeing fire. Some of them ran from my plane of vision. My place was with the young, handsome man. I am behind him. He was about to be overcome by the flames. He dove to the ground on his stomach facing uphill. I came around him and hit the ground directly in front of him facing downhill. I could feel the rocks crunch into my chest, the dust hitting my face with a sting, as I landed.

This wonderful, fearless young man and I were lying face to face, no farther apart than a few inches. I felt locked onto his brown eyes, which I can never forget. We could hear the flames approaching... the loud crackling of the burning bushes. My young partner kept looking into my eyes. He had no fear.

As the flames swept over us I spontaneously evacuated the premonition. I know he followed me out. I could feel him with me. That young heroic soul did not suffer from the flames because he left when I did.

From that point I do not know what transpired, as far as his continued transition and journey were concerned. But I do know he was not alone as he began his departure, and it was my honor to have been there. He wasn't alone. That wonderful young soul is somewhere out there being a hero, which is probably what he chooses to do in each incarnation.

This experience affected me profoundly and it was the first of its kind. I desperately didn't want to be the one who experiences this type of thing. I told people about the impossible premonition. It was impossible because, to my knowledge, firefighters never perish together. Two days later, in Colorado, was the South Canyon Fire on Storm King Mountain on July 6, 1994. It was known as the Storm King Fire.

Years later when the internet became a household tool, I researched this fire and found a picture of the fire crew and there I found the young man I had been with during the incident. I understand all too well the horrible nature of losing a loved one in this life. It hurts so deeply because we know we will not meet again for a long time. I recognize the sensitive nature of the firefighters experience and the pain the families feel at their loss. It was a profound honor to have accompanied this young man as he rose for his transition. He was prepared, brave and calm.

Second Experience

The next premonition has not yet happened, but if and when it does ... I know I was created for the important purpose of being there for another young man. This inner whisper/premonition opens with me sitting in the passenger side of a newer model military vehicle with no roof. There are two people in the rear seat, the driver, and myself on the passenger side. In front of us was a large enclosed military truck with ten wheels. After researching this I believe it to be an M35 2 ½ ton Army truck or a future model similar to that. There was also a truck behind us, the same as the one in front. I don't know if the convoy was larger than that, since all I saw was the three vehicles.

As is usually the case with me, I don't know where I was, yet it was warm and seemed to be a summer day. It felt comfortable, maybe around 75 degrees. We were heading north, driving down a two-lane asphalt-paved road. We were between two steep mountain ranges equal distance from the convoy, about a mile or so on each side. The sky was very blue with small nonthreatening clouds here and there.

The valley we were in was flat farmland. To the right of the road was green hay, and round hay bales placed neatly and evenly apart. Lining the road on the left, the west side , were mature, tall seasonal trees, placed evenly apart, they looked like cottonwood trees. Both sides of the road were fenced with farm-type fencing.

Now, leering up behind us, to our left, came a sound, faint and from a great distance. The sound alone was unnerving, and growing louder at a very quick rate. It was a single high-pitched tone, solid and unwavering with no distortion. Approaching at an extreme speed, it was carrying with it something frightening and dangerous. The body of the sound was nothing like a whistle of a bomb, in other words, the sound was not generated by a fast moving object ripping through the air's resistance; yet, it was more like the sound was self-generated and what it carried in it needed to be feared, nearing at a speed I can't understand. Very high pitched, but smooth and powerful ... it was sound with substance.

I could feel the apprehension filling my chest, like what you feel when you're being chased in the dark. But whatever was happening, was happening quickly.

Without turning to look back to see this unknown thing, I could clearly hear it surge over the peak of the mountains behind me, to the west. The shielding of the cliffs now gone, the ear-piercing wave brandished its unencumbered furry. Instead of looking back, I automatically hunched my shoulders, lifted my hands to my head and drew my knees to my chest.

The sound hit us and rolled over like a wave. As it did, I couldn't feel any heat, it wasn't carrying heat. It was doing something else. I think maybe it was speeding up the molecular structure of the objects and landscape and causing them to endure instant friction, leading to a very quick ignition. I also remember the grass was not at that time being affected. Just the objects sticking up from the ground.

To my right a hay bale blew up in flames, then another one ignited. Then the truck ahead of us exploded into flames, while simultaneously the tall-leaved trees started lighting off one after the other, Boom! Whoof! The truck behind us blew up. We were next, it was at that moment that the driver and I looked at each other. He was young, with a beautiful face, sharp check bones, looking at me from under his helmet. He had blue piercing eyes. The eye contact, the connection — and then I evacuated the vision.

If this premonition is unable to be avoided, I am comforted to know that in this realm, the young man will not be alone as his transition begins because I will be with him.

Third Experience

The third premonition I will share with you begins when I found myself standing on a two-lane road. It was during the day and the sun shone brightly. I felt as if I was facing south. Both sides of the road had wild grasses a couple of feet deep and the land there looked like Wyoming or Montana, however… it could have been anywhere with that kind of terrain.

I saw two men lying in the grass to my left. They were about 15 feet in front of me and off the road. Both men were white and probably in their 40s. As I walked over to them, the man closest to me was on his stomach and he wore blue jeans and a white shirt with a collar, so it was most likely one of those shirts that buttoned up the front. He had already transitioned. This man must have had another "earth angel" with him during his time.

The second man was on his back and he also wore jeans, a blue lightweight jacket that was open and a white t-shirt. His head was away from the road so he was lying angled down, just a little bit. He was still living. I walked to his side and sat down next to him and I settled close to his left shoulder, so I could easily see his face. I sat with my legs crossed and pulled up to my chest, so I could close my arms around my knees. He was of medium build, dark short hair, brown eyes and there were no unusual features to his face. I believe he didn't want to be there — alone at this time.

I sat there with him and we looked at each other for quite some time. He laid in the warm sun until the moment came when his body went to sleep and he was pulled from this place. There was no impending danger to me and I didn't need to evacuate the position, so I just sat with him and waited, and then he left. I know that the where and how of his leaving were a terrible loss to his loved ones. I wish I knew who he was, however, I do know he was NOT alone.

I don't know the cause of his death, whether it was a car wreck or some kind of foul play. I don't remember seeing a car and I could observe quite some distance in all directions. The grass we were resting in was of the kind that would break and lay flat when you sat on it. So I wonder if the imprint of where I was sitting was still there when the two men were finally discovered. Nonetheless, I am comforted to know that when I listen to my inner whispers, I know it is to go to bring comfort to someone who is transitioning to their next journey.

When I have these experiences I immediately bond with these individuals, during and following each incident. There are times I wish there was a way I could pin down a location or date in order to possibly intervene, but the nature of these events makes that impossible. This confirms to me that I am sent for a single purpose and that is the function I must perform. These people are already slated to move on to new adventures.

I have learned that if I am in the presence of someone in extreme peril and distress during these experiences, I am drawn to acquire eye contact with them, and I know that during this moment, no matter its position in the timeline, that we are seeing one another. I play a small role in their experience at that moment, but I also perceive that they know they are not alone. During the initiation of their transition they are not alone and the eye contact is too intense and clear to not be real. So at these moments, these people have the comfort of a witness and a companion as their transition begins.

There is usually some kind of time differential occurring because during my premonition I am with the individual as they begin passing, but in their timeline the incident has not yet happened. Since I am present in my premonition, I remain present when it circles around to them, even though my life has already moved forward from the time of my experience.

My greatest hope in this matter is that others, like me, have learned to listen to their inner whispers. As a result, everyone beginning their transition alone will be joined by someone, in whatever capacity, that can ease the anxiety and reassure them that they have a witness, a companion, who says silently, "I see you."

It matters not if, in this life, I know the person, because at that moment we are souls and we have always known each other. So I join them as a friend and witness. It is my prayer that my purpose in these precious moments is to help calm the initiation of their transition, so at that instance their loved ones and friends who wait for them on the other side can lift them from the moment, and their only experience then is Love.

Dedicated to my Granddaughter Harlo Monro (the sweetest little girl in my world) who reintroduced me to the gravity of life. To my two tiny dogs, Bell, my best friend and angel on Earth, and Bee, Bell's lively assistant. My father, Richard, who passed years ago, but has stayed to watch over me.

I am grateful to my mother, Lilas Hardin, for her many years of support and for helping me lay out this particular Chapter. I also want to thank Lisa Hardwick and Chelle Thompson of Visionary Insight Press for seeing who I am. I love the editing suggestions you made and I so appreciate you helping me get my message across accurately.

~ Catherine Madeira

It is always with excitement
that I wake up in the morning
wondering what my intuition
will toss up to me, like gifts
from the sea. I work with it and
rely on it. It's my partner.

~ JONAS SALK

Elizabeth Candlish

ELIZABETH CANDLISH is a passionate Teacher, Healer and Intuitive/ Medium, and loves to help others through healing sessions and teaching workshops. Helping people to achieve the life they were meant to live through healing and Life Coaching. She is a student of life, always learning and studying for the next level in her journey of life and inspiring others.

Elizabeth lives with her husband Martin on the beautiful Sunshine Coast in British Columbia, Canada. Elizabeth enjoys reading, gardening, knitting, writing, travelling and spending time with family and friends.

eacandlish@dccnet.com
elizabethcandlish.com

The Wings Of An Angel

 Those we love don't go away
They walk beside us every day
Unseen, unheard, but very near
Still loved, still missed and very dear.

~ AUTHOR UNKNOWN

It all began with a message I received from my mum in December 2014, through a lovely lady named Deborah, letting me know that she loved the short stories I was writing and to keep writing them. She affirmed that my shared experiences were helping others who were going through similar experiences. Although I had already decided to let my publisher know that I wouldn't be taking part in this book; on hearing this message from my mum, it gave me a sign that readers were finding it comforting during their own personal challenges.

How does my mum know this? I believe it is because she is around me and sees what is going on with myself and all our family — but what's more, she has the unique gift that only passed spirits are privileged with — the gift of seeing the bigger picture in certain parts of my life.

Do you believe in life after death?

Have you seen any white feathers lately, or maybe found dimes on the floor in an unexpected place? Have you ever sensed an energy through a familiar aroma that reminds you of that certain person — it is my belief that this is a sign and that they are letting us know that they are close by. These are just a few of the signs that our loved ones leave for us, to comfort us in the thought that they are watching over us, and are still with us even though we cannot see them.

Several years ago my mum had been going through tests, as she had a cough for quite a few weeks. They found some spots on her lungs through having an x-ray and then other tests. Eventually, she was diagnosed with lung cancer which was secondary, as it had spread from her kidneys.

My mum refused all treatments as she wanted to maintain a quality of life that the treatment, such as chemotherapy, would have reduced. We quickly found out, as a result of pain in her legs, that the cancer had spread to her bones. I immediately wanted to go over to the UK (I live in Canada) and look after her, but she refused my help at this time, being the independent woman that she was. She phoned to let me know that she was okay and agreed that I would be able to offer better support later on.

Knowing that I wasn't going over there any time soon, I did what I do best and sent distance healing to her. Being a Reiki Master/ Teacher/ Practitioner, I felt comfort in the fact that I could use my skills to help alleviate her symptoms. Back in the UK, my sisters, who lived close by, both helped our mum as best they could, and as a team, we were connected through helping to care for her.

It really is amazing what distance healing can do. I always knew when my mum had a bad night or a good night. My sisters could never understand how I knew these things, but I did through connecting with her energy whilst sending her distance healing.

One Saturday my sister phoned and said my mum had been rushed to the hospital, as she had fluid on the lungs and wasn't going to survive the night. The hospital was going to drain her lungs that evening and I told her that I felt that my mum would wake up in the morning and wonder what all the fuss was about, and that is exactly what she did and was sent home a couple of days later. How did I know? In my opinion, we had generated a metaphysical connection through the power of Reiki.

This was confirmation for me that I was helping her. By sending distance healing to her every evening as she slept, her body benefited from a deeply relaxing energy source, and connected the two of us in ways I couldn't imagine possible.

It wasn't long before I received "the" phone call. A day or two later I flew over to the UK. I arrived on Saturday and my mum was pleased to see me and we ate lunch together. I was told later by family that she had hardly eaten anything, as her appetite was hugely affected at this time, so to see her eat anything and be eager about it, was good news. This surge of appetite was, however, short lived, as unfortunately by the next day she wouldn't eat anything.

I wanted to help as much as I could and never left the house, not even for a minute, as I wanted to be there for her in any way I could — whether it was bathing, helping her to eat or to have sips of water, or just simply to hold her hand.

The nurses came by several times a day to give my mum her medication and to see how she was doing. We also had the McMillan Nurses coming in and staying overnight so that we could all try and get some rest.

My mum was sleeping downstairs in her bed, as by this time, she was bedridden and in a coma. While I was sleeping upstairs in her bed (above the room where she was now sleeping), I recall one evening that I was awakened by someone coughing. I listened and it came again and again. It was my mum downstairs. I got up and went downstairs and found that the nurse had fallen asleep. I said to my mum "It's okay. I'm going to stay with you now. You're not alone." It is my belief that my mum was letting me know that she did not want to die on her own. I sat with her for over an hour when the nurse eventually woke up. She was surprised to see me when she woke, thinking she'd only fallen asleep for a few minutes and not the hour or so I had witnessed.

She started to explain her reasons for sleeping on the job, but I was annoyed with her, as it had been a comfort to the family to believe someone was watching our mum, so we could each get some sleep in order to care for her in the day. I was glad I heard my mum and went to her side to comfort her. Even though she was in a coma, she still had her ways of being heard. She let me know that she felt alone and I was happy to be there for her.

Mum was a very determined woman indeed. She had waited for me to come and see her for the last time, and now she was waiting for her granddaughter to return from holiday with her family. A couple of days later, her granddaughter came straight from the airport to say her goodbyes.

The following day we were told that she only had hours to live. So my sister and I never left her side and my younger sister joined us a few hours later.

My sisters sat on either side of my mum holding her hands, and I was at her feet sending her Reiki and wishing for a peaceful passing for her. She was in no pain as her medication and Reiki eased this part of her final hours.

We told her that it was okay to go and not to worry about us as we would all take care of each other. Sometimes, loved ones, need permission to go and want reassurance that everyone will be okay.

My mum passed away at 7PM on the Wednesday evening, very peacefully, surrounded by her daughters and that is the way she wanted it to be.

She had said to us that she wanted no tears around her bed. This was so hard to do but we were able to grant her that. When she had passed, we let the tears flow.

As you can imagine we were all deeply upset. Even though you know someone is going to pass away, it can still come as a shock.

We were all busy over the next few days organizing the funeral, flowers and service. The evening before the funeral I asked Archangel Michael to put the protection around me. I wanted everything to go smoothly and peacefully for her funeral.

As I stood at the graveside I was very emotional. Tears ran down my face as I threw a rose onto her coffin, then suddenly out of nowhere, I felt as if someone had put a huge cloak around my shoulders. I felt the weight of it. I was so surprised I looked around to see if anyone had seen anything, because it felt so real, and to me, it was real. At that moment all emotion stopped and I felt completely calm and at peace. As I thought about it, I realized that Archangel Michael had answered my prayer for help. He had put *his* wings around me to protect, comfort and support me through this challenging moment. I was then turned around and guided away from the burial ground and on to the car with my sisters.

Thank you Archangel Michael. I always know you will be there, when your assistance is requested.

About 10 days later, after I arrived home, I was driving along a quiet road. There were no trees around, only blue sky. The day was very clear and sunny with no wind. As I was reaching the junction, two white feathers intertwined, came down and landed on my windshield. I smiled. I knew that my mum and dad were back together again. One feather for each of them, travelling together once more.

Loved ones and angels are always with us. We just need to be conscious of the signs they leave us and have confidence in their lasting energy. We only have to ask for their help and it will be there.

When Tomorrow Starts Without Me

When tomorrow starts without me
And I'm not there to see;
If the sun should rise and find your eyes
All filled with tears for me.

I wish so much you wouldn't cry
The way you did today;
While thinking of the many things
We didn't get to say.

I know how much you love me
As much as I love you;
And each time that you think of me
I know you'll miss me too.

When tomorrow starts without me
Don't think we're far apart
For every time you think of me
I'm right here in your heart.

~ DAVID ROMANO

(Excerpted from "Chicken Soup for the Teenage Soul")

To my mum, thank you for your message, and encouraging me to continue writing short stories.

We both did the best we could with the knowledge and experience we had; but at the end of the day we loved each other to the end and beyond.

~ Elizabeth Candlish

Janine Forder

JANINE FORDER is an intuitive healer and combines her love of people and the Spirit world to connect the dots. She runs her own business helping people get Back2Love as a Flower Remedy Practitioner, Mind Calm Meditation Coach, Animal Communicator and Spiritual Response Therapy Practitioner. She is also writing a book about her journey and everyday interactions with a Rock Star Angel.

Janine lives in Glenlivet in Scotland with her Husband and six cats where she is able to relax into BEing or play her music too loud, depending on her mood!

www.back2love.me

From Kittens to
❧ Rock Star Angels

Have you ever thought *"It would be useful to know the difference between my own ramblings in my head and true Intuition (Universal Truth)?"* Me too. The answer is to TRUST, and here's my story of how I'm being helped every day by a Rock Star Angel (no, seriously!) to understand *HOW* to trust.

I'm being shown how to *trust* my intuition, my inner voice, my support network, the Universe, and how to *trust* I am on the right path. My Rock Star Angel tells me that *"intuition is a process which happens in your subconscious when it recognizes one of your soul family or when you enter into a situation that's in line with your divine purpose. Your Higher Self (your Soul) recognizes the connection with the person or the situation as "meant to be", so you can take action and act upon your intuition. So you see, intuition is the recognition of Universal Truth."* The biggest challenge for most of us is what to do with this intuition and how to trust it.

It's rare any of us truly appreciate how far we've come. This is in part because when we start opening up to question our life purpose, we tend to be looking forward. It's also because our journey has not been one big trek, but has been made up of lots of individual steps and short walks, and the odd jog. We've already trusted ourselves and the Universe so many times to get to where we are today, we just might not know it.

The more I learn about my own spiritual journey, the more I find myself in situations where I'm around a table with people (mainly women) being asked about what I do, how I connect with Spirit, what I believe in and why. All of them are curious, and want to know how they tap into and use their own intuition to drive their lives forward. And they usually have a couple of questions for me;

1) *"How do I know that these nudges or messages are not all in my head?"*

2) *"How do you know these messages aren't just your own mind or that this Rock Star Angel, or any other spirit is real?"*

In essence these two questions are identical. The first is about *them* feeling scared and unsure of their own *perceived* abilities to use their intuition; the second is an extension of this doubt, and an appeal for *me* to prove something to them, to show them how it works.

Any lightworker has this sort of test at some point, where they feel they have to prove themselves and their skills to someone. I've been on my own journey over the last six months with this second question. Because of my fear of being judged, I used to think people were asking with a sense of skepticism and an air of "come on then, show me how, give me proof..." I have been in situations where I interpreted this question negatively and I felt ridiculed. In a way it helped, as it pushed me closer to my Rock Star Angel, and he kept asking me to trust him more with all sorts of aspects of my life. So I did, and he rewarded me by showing me the truth. He's put me into many (unexpected) safe environments with loving people who made me feel comfortable enough to talk openly and share our story. He's shown me how people are genuinely curious and have a real and true thirst for the answers. I had that thirst in me when I started to realize there was more to life than the human day to day existence. It started 12 years ago; and all because of a kitten...

I had been through a rough patch, and I felt a deep sense of loss. Within a few months, my mother had moved to another country, I'd had animals and my Nan die and I didn't know how to cope. Two major and positive things happened to me as a result of these losses.

1) I discovered the Bach Flower Remedies, initially to help our cats who were grieving the loss of one of their siblings. I am delighted to say I subsequently qualified as a Flower Remedy Practitioner, and I now choose remedies for people intuitively, trusting my instincts on which remedies they need by literally tuning into them, and grabbing the right remedies. They are always spot on.

2) I stumbled upon a new friend who introduced me to Spiritual "stuff" and started my process of self-discovery (which I'm still on). This process has changed my life completely and now I communicate regularly with Spirit, and live with a Rock Star Angel by my side, day in, day out, as well as my (wonderful and patient) husband!

Here's what happened. Hubby and I had decided we wanted another cat so I looked through the local newspaper adverts, but none really stood out to me. My husband said *"just call the person with that advert there — yes I know they don't have what we're after — but I have a feeling"*, so I made the call and enquired about the kittens she was offering. The lady (named Shauneen) told me they'd all been rehomed but she had others which were just one week old and it was touch and go as to whether they'd survive according to the vet. She said for me to call in eight weeks when they'd be ready, if they lived.

When I got off the phone, I had a REAL urge that I needed to go and see these tiny kittens anyway. This nudge felt fluttery, exciting, and I felt almost desperate. The urge became overwhelming and for the first time in my consciously aware adult life I took action on an inner knowing — on my intuition — and called her straight back. *"Look, I know this is going to sound really stupid, but I've got a feeling about your kittens, can I come to see them now?"*

Little did either of us know then, that this phone call would change BOTH our lives! And this is how Spirit works, dear reader, because as I wrote that, I was informed by Shauneen's late husband Allan that it was he who changed our lives, as he made the phone call happen. (Allan was a medium whilst he was alive, and he just popped in to tell me this — he's as cheeky as my Rock Star Angel!) This is how Spirit works with us and our intuition. If we're missing something vital and not quite connecting the dots, they're on board to help us and will nudge and sometimes shove us in the right direction. I am glad they do!

My hubby and I clicked instantly with Shauneen (not surprising as I now know we have had many a past life together in every relationship type imaginable — remember I said your soul knows when you meet your soul family? This was one of those times). We chatted for hours. We also fell in love with these two little kittens that chose us by climbing up our legs.

Shauneen mentioned she was desperate for a job. I knew my employers were hiring people to sell IT products into companies. I asked *"do you know anything about computers?"* and it turns out she'd once been a sales person, and then retrained as a computer programmer, so yes, yes she did! To cut a long story short, she had a job working with me a week later and we soon became very close friends.

It turned out the day before we met, Shauneen had done a Tarot reading for herself, and the card in her 'possible immediate future' position said to "be aware of help from unexpected sources" — us! You never know what's around the corner so never lose hope. This message has carried me forward through so many tough times, and the right person to help has always shown up, with the right message at the right time. As I pondered what story I should share with you, one of Shauneen's "kittens" (now 12 years old) came and stood on my laptop. She gave me the nudge — the reminder that it was getting her that started my conscious foray into being Awake. This is what I mean, messages come from all over; from Spirit, intuition, and even from cats!

The spiritual things Shauneen was into really piqued my interest and I asked her so many questions about spirituality, intuition, crystals, Angels, the lot; just as people do with me today. In fact, I asked her the same questions *"how do I connect with Spirit, and how do I know it's not all in my head?"* I can assure you, the idea that you could talk to dead people (Spirit) was overwhelming and just felt so far out of reach, and was certainly a road I didn't want to go down. Well it seemed my soul, and the Universe, had other ideas...

Shauneen bought me the Doreen Virtue Archangel Oracle cards and I started out by choosing one each morning to help me through the day. And when I applied the messages, my day went pretty well and so I wanted to connect more with the Angels because it seemed to be working.

The more I tried to connect, the more things shifted. It doesn't matter HOW you try, because when you are aligning with your purpose, even if you don't know what that is, you *will* be shown the right way. It is like you're transmitting a radio signal to the Universe which says *"I'm getting on the right wavelength, plug me in."* Intention counts.

I started asking the Angels directly for help, but I soon got cross because I didn't feel my requests were being answered. I mean, if you write *"Dear Angels, please stop this person being a bitch toward me"*, you expect something to change, right? And not only that, how come all I then got was a load of signs and repetitive messages (things on the TV, things I read etc.) reminding me that when you point the finger, look at where the other fingers are pointing—back at you. Cue epiphany moment: "Oh yeah..." It dawned on me that I was being reminded that my request for help was focused on the negative, and that I needed to take responsibility for my own part in creating this situation I was so unhappy with, where I felt bullied.

I changed my request *"Dear Angels, please help her to feel more secure, and for me to behave in a way that makes her feel better so she's nicer toward me"* and it worked! I was shown that when I ask for help IN THE RIGHT WAY, not interfering with anyone else's free will—and crucially by focusing on love—it worked.

Messages from Angels, Spirits and intuition *feel* similar. You know you've had a divine message when you get an idea or feeling and it's like you've had a whole conversation or long drawn out plan but it's just there in your head, in an instant. This is pretty handy really, as it means you also don't have to wait as long to get a lot of knowledge, as you would if you had to learn it in human time! The more messages I got, the more I trusted. The more I trusted, the more Spirit-related things started to happen.

After about three weeks of being woken up every morning at 4.22am by faces in the dark, I was scared stiff, a bag of nerves and completely frazzled. I know so many people who say *"I want to develop my intuition and grow, but I don't want to talk to dead people and start seeing things."* If this is how you feel, *please don't panic* because spiritual development and tuning into your intuition doesn't mean you lose control. All it means is once you open yourself up to the vibrations of Universal Energy, you become aware of, and better able to connect with everything within that energy, and this includes Spirits and Angels. We are all one. You'll have seen that written before, well this is what it means. There is no us and them, dead or alive, we're all just energy. We are made of the same stuff — Universal Energy.

One day at work, Shauneen said to me *"You look exhausted — are you ok?"* I burst into tears and told her what was going on. *"It can't be real, I'm not a bloody child, how can I see faces in the dark?"* Thankfully she knew how to help. She was friends with a medium who taught me how to manage the spirit visits, and how to protect myself, to stay grounded and eventually how to channel spirits if I chose to. I didn't want to talk to dead people either at that time, and didn't know why I was being shown how to do it, but boy, am I so glad I *did* learn!

If you'd have told me back then that I would be talking every day to Spirit, having the time of my life, smiling because of a Spirit, my Rock Star Angel, I would have laughed in your face. I mean don't get me wrong, I'd have also thought it sounded pretty cool, but I wouldn't have thought it was something I could ever, or would ever want to do. But that's because I didn't realize that communicating with this Spirit could plug me straight into Source, that Universal Energy. I do know my journey is my own, and that of the Rock Star Angel is his own, and I also know we're intrinsically linked and always have been. I know we're here to bring out the (Universal) best in each other, as are you with your soul family. You, too, have your own direct link into the Universal Energy and it's already there within you. Feel that? It's your Higher Self, that part of you that knows when something feels right and that trusts, even when you can't see the path ahead.

Send out your own transmission to the Universe and watch the response. It could be a song you keep hearing or maybe you have these ideas that just appear in your head. You may get the same message a few times over, or little niggles to make that change. Or perhaps *your* next step is hidden just around the corner, ready to come to you when you least expect it, but when it is just right to fit in with your divine plan. Trust.

Dedicated to Simon, my loving husband, my wonderful friend Shauneen (and her husband Allan). You have always supported my growth and believed in me, and loved me throughout every experience. Thank you both for your pure and unconditional love. I am looking forward to the rest of this life together, and the lifetimes yet to come. I love you.

I am so grateful to everyone I've met along my journey, especially the Soul Family I've been with in many a lifetime — you've all taught me so much and will continue to for many lifetimes! These special friends include Naomi Tamayama, Curtis Michaels, Kerry Allen, Bridget Mary-Clare, Brad Simkins, Nicola McQueen, Sheryl Newman and Hilary Laverty. And of course, to my Rock Star Angel, you make this part of my journey so much fun, and your encouragement, love, friendship and ability to keep me light of heart and always safe, mean so much to me.

~ Janine Forder

All human knowledge thus begins
with intuitions, proceeds thence
to concepts, and ends with ideas.

~ IMMANUEL KANT

Donna Jutras Tobey

DONNA JUTRAS TOBEY is passionate about living limitless possibilities out loud while teaching others how to do the same! She is a personal coach, mentor, workshop teacher, writer, and speaker. She is trained, certified, and licensed as a **Heal Your Life**® Workshop Teacher and Coach, based on the philosophies of Louise L. Hay.

Donna lives in Somersworth, New Hampshire, with her son, Ian and her two lively Maine coon cats, Arty and Ditey. All three boys keep her laughing! She is founder of *You've Got the Power, Baby!* inspiring everyone to find their answers WITHIN.

Mostly, she is a student of Life who allows Divine Intelligence to be her teacher!

ugotpowerbaby.com

🌿 Look for the Life!

The sky was an ominous dark purplish gray; the ground wet below my feet. It was quiet, very early morning, chilly. As I sifted and sorted through the cold wet sand, I noticed another family at the other end of the beach — seemed to be a mom, dad and two kids. They too were sifting and sorting. The storm the night before had churned up what was hidden deep below its cold ocean floor; treasures waiting to be discovered!

Whispering loving words to the abundant ocean before me, I was admiring its great depth and vast beauty. Lost in the relish of this powerful creation, mystical, home of many secrets, filled with magnificent life. My heart, listening to the soothing peaceful lullaby of the waves coming in and going out, fills with deep gratitude for its presence in my life. As if responding right on cue, I spy a tiny glistening green heart-shaped piece of sea glass, ever so sweetly waiting for me to discover it. My heart squeals in delight! Love from the Universe, the perfect symbol of giving and receiving, just as the waves rush in to give and the tide flows back to receive.

"Look for the life!" my heart whispers. I am listening, my mind wondering what that means. "Look for the life in all of life's experiences!" A little more is whispered.

"Everybody, come see what I have found, you aren't going to believe it!" an excited young voice shouts out to his family. Curious, I wander over to see what gift the Universe bestowed upon him. Treasure! O, the possibilities!

Shivering, with the palm of his hand wide open, is a ten-year-old boy admiring a generous piece of amethyst. One side rock-like, rough, bumpy; the other side sparkly purple, pointy, glistening, alive. He asks me if I know what this treasure is.

As he is listens, his eyes sparkle in sheer delight, taking it all in. "Today is my tenth birthday!" he shares in his exuberance.

My heart smiles widely and I respond, "You have been given a precious gift! Happy birthday to you." *Life*.

The whispers of my heart always ask me to look for the life in each of life's experiences. I have come to understand more of its meaning each and every day. As life unfolds its treasure to me one day at a time, I know that my perception and how I receive its precious gifts are entirely up to me. Yes, you heard right, *gifts*.

The other choice would be obstacles, challenges, difficulties. "Opportunities" is what my heart whispers to me; choice. The chance to choose life yet again! An opportunity to learn from past experiences and choices; a chance to choose differently. Learning from my past which experiences brought more life, as well as what didn't quite work out the way I had intended. Arms wide open, I am willing to receive this great gift simply for the opportunity to choose again.

Life will always bring you what you need to learn right now. It will continue to gift you with that moment to make some change in your perspective, to view a situation differently, examine what you believe. How you receive and how you perceive makes all the difference. Will you receive calmly, gently, in a peaceful, tender way? Will you "look for the life," asking to be shown what good will come from this situation? Will you see past what is right in front of you and beyond to the bigger picture?

Will you perceive this life experience as an opportunity to grow, to meet new people, to learn something you never knew? Will you perceive this experience as the precious gift it is to move you one step closer to an abundant, joyful and joy-filled life? Will you say "thank you" for another chance to choose, even when you cannot see the outcome? Will you trust that only good will come from this experience?

Just as the ocean's tides ebb and flow, giving and receiving, life is always giving, waiting for you to receive that treasure it is giving you each and every moment of every day: your own magnificence! Do you see it? Can you feel it? Yes, it is that treasure that is **YOU**!

Love the One You're With!

Learning to cultivate that one-on-one relationship with yourself opens many doors to opportunity and new life. Often we are entirely too busy caring for others to take any time for what makes us feel alive and thrive! It's time. Give yourself permission to spend time alone, to reconnect to those pieces of you that you have tucked away waiting for the "right" time to live. The right time is NOW: this present moment.

It takes time and commitment to learn about you. It's a practice of learning to love yourself just the way you are. Did you know that there's a part of your soul that lives in your heart called the Subconscious Self? You may have heard of it referred to as your Inner Child. It is that little three-year-old child that lives within you. It is in charge of running the systems of your body, storing memories, and is that emotional part of you, which can be irrational just like a little child.

Have you connected with your inner three-year-old lately? If you're feeling emotional about your life and experiences, perhaps it's time. There's some communication that wants to be expressed to you. Every time we cry without really knowing the reason why, a call is being sent out for you to pay attention. Are you listening?

Loving yourself takes practice. Listening to the whispers of your own heart also takes practice. Start by putting your right hand on your heart, closing your eyes and taking three deep breaths. Then ask your inner child if there's anything you need to know right now. Lastly, simply *listen*.

 Affirm: Every day I tune in to the whispers of my own heart by deliberately making time to listen.

Baby, You Were Born This Way!

Did you know that there is no other person just like you? It's true. You are unique in your own right. Sometimes we feel like we just don't fit in, don't fit the mold, aren't like everyone else. That's because we're not. You are uniquely **YOU**. Period.

It takes many of us years to begin to understand and appreciate the gifts that we have within us. We are born with gifts and talents that we are in charge of bringing into this world. Yes, you are very special in that way AND so is everyone else. Many times we cannot see our gifts and talents, they may seem hidden from us. Look closer, they are there.

As you start to look back on your life's journey, you may recognize that there's a similar pattern in your life experience. You keep attracting the same types of situations over and over again. We repeat a similar looping of experience in a slightly different way. You will begin to identify your strengths and your weaknesses. What comes easy to you? What seems natural? It's funny how many of our perceived weaknesses end up really being our strengths!

Are you able to see the value that your past life experience provided for you as a way to develop new life skills? Are you using some of these skills in your day-to-day life right now? Take a moment to examine the life skills you have gained along the way. Make a list if that helps you. It's important that you see just how many gifts and talents you have developed and ways you are using these skills in your life; likely helping others too.

Affirm: I am one of a kind! Uniquely designed for what I bring into this world.

Who Are You?

Choices you make help to define the kind of life you are living. How do you feel about your life? Do you love it? How are you investing your precious life-force energy? Are you *choosing* to do what you love, and love what you do?

Thoughts and words actually CREATE. There is a creative energy or original substance that surrounds us and responds to our dominant thoughts and words. This energy is referred to by many names: Source Energy, Divine Intelligence, the Universe, God and Creator, to name a few. What you are temporarily living right now is the results of those thoughts and words that set in motion a response from this creative life-force energy. I use the word "temporarily" because everything in this world is in constant motion; ever changing.

The GREAT news is, it's only a thought and a thought can be changed. This means that your temporary life experience can also be changed by making changes to your dominant thoughts and words. *Pay attention!* Are you thinking and speaking in words that come from lack — or abundance?

Abundant thoughts and words are loving, kind and supportive. They speak of more LIFE. They affirm and acknowledge that limitless possibilities exist and surround us all the time; miracles every day, all day. They have depth and the qualities of wealth, whether it is wealth of money, wealth of time, wealth of friends, wealth of family, or wealth of opportunities. These thoughts fulfill the soul deeply, filling your heart with profound love and appreciation.

Choose your thoughts and words wisely. Make sure what you desire is what you are thinking about and speaking about. Let go of past life experiences that want to tell you something has to be a certain way. Create the life you want to live. It requires persistence and practice. But remember, it's only a thought and a thought can be changed!

 Affirm: I create a new life with new rules that totally support me.

Clowns to the Left of Me, Jokers to the Right

Every one of us likely knows a few people who just seem to create one problem after another in their lives, never ending! More than that, they feel compelled to bring us right into the midst of their chaos. Because we are compassionate and care about our friends and family, it's very easy to get pulled into their drama. But at some point, we need to question if this is a good investment of our energy.

Though it takes much practice, learning to pull yourself out of the lives of others is really a necessity. It doesn't mean that we don't care. As a matter of fact, our choosing to not join them in their continued mis-creations actually helps them. Less talking about the same old, same old; creating the same old, same old. Instead invest your energy in thinking about all the pure, positive potential that this person has right at their fingertips, should they choose to receive it. Come from a place of compassion and an inner knowing that whatever they are temporarily experiencing is not the Truth about them.

The Truth is, continually joining someone in their suffering is nothing but a distraction keeping us from paying attention to our own lives. If we focus our attention on someone else's life, we are not paying attention to our own. We cannot change someone else's life. Only they can do that. They are the co-creators of their own lives, just as we are in ours.

By paying attention to how we invest our energy, we make a difference not only to ourselves, but also to others. We are each responsible for the ways we invest our money, time and support of others in this world. Are we supporting life? Are we saying yes to our passions? Are we investing our money in ways that offer opportunities to others? Are we being responsible for the way we use our thoughts and words?

Letting others live their lives the way they see fit, accepting people where they are in their growth, is a valuable gift to give them. Realize that we each have been given this amazing life to live. Live yours and let others live theirs peacefully. Respect each other, be kind and loving to each other, and allow each other to create his or her own magnificent life!

 Affirm: I am wisely investing my own energy in ways that make a difference for everyone by focusing on my own life.

Sweet Child O' Mine

Remember what you loved to do as a child? What occupied most of your time? What were you passionate about? Was there a certain song you loved to listen to? Was there a certain place you most felt alive? Do you find yourself nostalgic at times, wishing those days were still here?

Everything in life happens for a reason. Look to your early childhood for activities that delighted you. Put yourself in that memory and really tune in to the substance of this memory. Feel the joy that kept you interested for hours; tap into that feeling of discovery and creation. How can you recreate this same passionate, joyful feeling now? Perhaps you could start a project similar to what you did as a child. Dig out that old music and crank it! Take a road trip and visit that place that brought you such love. Once in that creative happy space, take a moment to dream about what your heart desires. Use that creative happy space to create even more.

Affirm: The JOY of my youth paves the way to the JOY of my life!

Gimme All Your Lovin'

It seems a silly question, but do you love yourself? For most of us, our automatic response is, "Of course I do!" But when you take a closer look, you may find that you really have not been your own best friend. I am always surprised when I hear someone call himself "stupid." I cringe inside when I hear it, but it rolls off many tongues without any thought.

Once I read a magazine that asked, "Do you treat yourself the same way you treat a beloved friend?" Good question. Positive self-talk and encouragement are keys to loving yourself. Your inner child, that three-year-old that is your Subconscious Self, is listening to every word, especially from you.

Mirror work is a great way for you to practice extreme self-care. It involves looking in your own eyes and saying loving words to yourself. Start with, "I love you, I really love you." Pay attention and notice if you look away or falter over the words or start thinking of something else, instead of being present. It's okay. It can feel ridiculous at first!

Positive words used as positive affirmations or declarations have a way of filling your own heart with love. If you start your day saying loving and passionate words to yourself, your spirit soars! You're ready for whatever the day may bring. Empower yourself and look to yourself for encouragement and kind words. Before long, you will be playfully creating fun things to say to yourself. You may even start to wink at yourself every time you pass a mirror!

Affirm: Every time I pass a mirror, I look into my own eyes, my own soul and see that Divine magnificent expression of life!

Don't Look Back

Your point of power is always in this present moment of NOW. Looking back to the past of what might have been, where you went wrong, regretting parts of your life, keeps you stuck. You can't do anything about it. It's over and done.

Today you have an opportunity to choose again. Every day, life will present you with new chances to live life joyfully! The choices you make today, right now, will bring about the positive changes you desire. Your life is ever changing, moment by moment. Challenge yourself to make one small change in your routine, do something different. Mix it up. Eat breakfast for dinner and dinner for breakfast, if that's all you can come up with *right now*.

Be grateful for where you have been and where you are going. You may even want to start a Gratitude Journal to write down five things you are grateful for each day. Some days it may be very difficult. Those are the days you'll need to push yourself to stay with it. Gratitude opens the way for more wonderful things to come your way. Look for the life, even and especially when, you don't feel like it.

 Affirm: I'm grateful to be alive in these exciting times of change!

No Matter What

No matter where you go, no matter what you do, there is an invisible support system in place that guides, guards and protects you. Every one of us has evidence and examples of this surrounding creative energy at work in our lives. That near miss, that situation that should have been deadly, that unexplained person who showed up just at the right moment. It defies logic in most cases. And yet, it happened.

Working in partnership with this creative life Source puts you in a flow of synchronistic life experiences, that some would call miracles. This happens every day, all day, whether you are aware of it or not. It does not just happen in the lives of those who are "lucky"; it happens in all of our lives. Think of Creator as an equal-opportunity giver!

Different results are experienced by different people depending on their level of willingness to give and to receive. We talked about perspectives and beliefs. How limiting are they? Are you resistant to any part of receiving your own gifts and talents? Your own inner being, inner wisdom, or Divine Intelligence, also known as your Higher Self, wants to give the abundance of the Universe to you.

Sadly, we won't believe that. Sadly, we think we are undeserving. Sadly, we deny that this is even possible. Sadly, we believe that the riches of life are finite. Sadly, we create prisons of our own making by squandering our gifts, not sharing. That synchronistic flow of life, giving and receiving, stops.

The great news is, we can shift our perceptions, beliefs and limitations and unlock the door to this self-imposed prison because we are the one who holds the key! Make a different choice. Let go of limited thoughts and belief systems. Be willing to open your heart and your mind to receive the TRUTH about life, the Truth about YOU.

Affirm: I am willing to break through the prison of my own making by changing the limiting ways in which I see and live life!

I Can See Clearly Now

The truth is that we have all done the best we could at any moment in our lives. There are many influences that have created our perceptions and beliefs; our life experience is our biggest point of reference. Strategies that worked out well and those that did not. As children, we subconsciously took on the beliefs of our parents, teachers, friends, family. Each influence was colored by that person's own life experiences.

As adults, now we have the opportunity to take a real look at some of these limitations. Are they even ours? Are we just buying into this belief because we learned it as a child? Are we listening to the scare tactics on television that tell us about the latest disease in the world? Are we scaring ourselves into submission and giving our agreements to these limiting factors? Is it what WE really believe?

So, what DO you believe? Do you believe it is our birthright to suffer? Do you believe that the Universe is selective in creating the haves and have nots, as many folks believe? Do you believe you have no choice and that you are a victim in your own life, powerless? Do you believe that the life you are living right now is the best it is ever going to be?

These are questions you will want to ask yourself. Even after you ask yourself and receive your answer, you will want to ask other questions. Where did this belief come from? Why do I believe that? Is it fear? Am I afraid to claim my own power to create? What am I gaining by holding on to these beliefs?

There is another player in this miraculous team in our own hearts, and it is called the Conscious Self. It is that inner adult who lives in this present moment of *now*. The Conscious Self is the one making decisions in your life. It is that very logical thinking part of you that wants logical answers to everything. It can also be that part of you that keeps you stuck.

Challenge yourself to see and be seen! Keep questioning the answers until you uncover what your heart knows to be true. Find the courage within to take that first right step to change, even if it is a little baby step. Encourage your Higher Self, Conscious Self and Subconscious Self to work together in supportive ways. Any change you make is a step closer to you. See yourself for who you truly are!

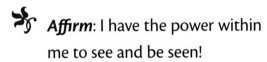 *Affirm*: I have the power within
me to see and be seen!

Roam Where You Want To

Trust the whispers of your own heart to know the way in your life. By design, you have been assigned leadership. It's your life to lead wherever you desire. Shift perceptions that keep you stuck and look for the life in every life experience you live. It is there.

Life is meant to be lived. It is meant to expand your awareness and consciousness and to fulfill your every desire! Be exuberant, embrace this adventure, find the thrill of everyday life, and test the boundaries that you have put in place. Life is not meant to contain you.

Trust life to lead you. There is no right or wrong way to live it; everything is perspective. The Truth is the Universe loves you no matter what. Choose wisely. Invest in ways that promote more life in the daily unfolding of your life. Be that wide-eyed, wondrous child ready to receive from an ever-abundant parent. Then give from the depth of your heart, sharing the jewels that you find.

Affirm: My heart knows the way to my dreams.
I receive its wisdom, knowing the way!

You are as powerful as the deep, vast, mysterious, magnificent ocean! Abundant and filled with new life! A treasure trove just waiting to be discovered. Dive deep into the still waters of your own heart. Be willing to receive the pearls of wisdom it has to gift you. Claim the treasure that is **YOU!**

Dedicated to my son, Ian Daniel Tobey, my greatest teacher.

Thank you God, thank you! Deep gratitude to my family and friends who fill my life with such JOY and many of my life's lessons. Each one of you is invaluable to the personal growth in my life, each one priceless! Special thanks to my former husband, Dana Tobey, for the many blessings and memories we share; to Scott Ferreira for sharing his friendship, gifts, talents, and co-founding Divine Light Society; and to Rick Pickford for seeing and capturing the essence of my beauty when I was not able.

~ Donna Jutras Tobey

Trust your own instinct. Your mistakes might as well be your own, instead of someone else's.

~ BILLY WILDER

Brenda Penn

BRENDA PENN started her career as a public service worker and later became an entrepreneur in small businesses and an active community member and volunteer. On the business side she developed and managed a cleaning business for residential and commercial business, and later in her career with her management background she moved into building management for larger companies. She rallied and pulled her block together and became captain of *your street plus adjoining street*, her activism and leadership for Block Watch Society of British Columbia was recognized within the community. Her study and research in a variety of spiritual modalities has both enriched and enlightened Brenda with daily meditation and self-discovery. Brenda holds the first and second degree in Usui System and is practicing Reiki healing while pursuing her masters in natural healing.

Brenda lives on the West Coast of Vancouver Island near the great Capital City of British Columbia, Victoria, with her life partner Brad Harper and children near.

issitterable@gmail.com

What Love Has to Do with Life

 "Of all the Whispers great and small
in the wondrous Mind we think it All."

~ BRENDA PENN

Whatever your intention is, it can be having the reverse effect you planned. It is really hard to know exactly what you are trying to accomplish because there is no communication about your plan. It is through your energy and vibration in the home that this is being felt.

I'm able to distinguish something different because you are different, your actions don't match your intentions and it's making me feel sick; I'm fighting with all my might to not react.

It seems like you're trying to change me with your inadvertent action — meaning non-communication — and it's not working. I just want to be Happy, learning how to take care of the things that need to be done as they arise, without the nonverbal judgement and chattering thoughts.

I see you for all of three hours a day and I'm thinking of ways to run away because I don't want this low energy. It vibrates at a sickly, unconscious level and it's making me ill.

My spirit and soul are suffering from the lack of Love; my body is wearing out because it feels your daily negative intention and non-verbal communication. I just want to run away and be with people who show affection from their spirit and soul-likeminded people who give back, where I can feel my energy rise and my spirit and soul sparkle with the light of life. Love!

I'm going to stop doing for you all the domestic duties that are being judged, the daily activities of domesticated living will be done with the enjoyment of filling life with love as it should be. Do you love making your house a home? Loving the realm and loving yourself through one day at a time shows up in everything we think and do. Slow down and get out of the rat race; get out of your own way. Life is not meant to be so hard that there is only hardness, sickly battling for every nice feeling we have and for Love.

And so it is.

From Influenced to Enlightenment

 "Learn to Give Expression to what you feel without blaming. Learn to listen to your partner in an open, non-defensive way. Give your partner space for expressing himself or herself. Be present. Accusing, defending, attacking — all those patterns that are designed to strengthen or protect the ego or to get its needs met will then be redundant. Giving space to others — and to yourself — is vital. Love cannot flourish without it."

~ ECKHART TOLLE

While being non-reactive we really are hurting ourselves because if we have to be a certain way, then that is a reaction and it lowers our vibration and takes away from being truly present. Any person living in a defensive/reactive life will always be challenged, within the mindset of duality. The spirit and soul become dull, the body runs on auto pilot, this is not living a life from Love. I need life to live through what I am. Stay strong, valuing yourself goes with the natural flow, as though you're dancing with life and sprinkling love with every step.

A Secret Was Whispered

I will never forget the day a very wise teacher, she is the wife of a Chief, whispered while sitting and doing her art ever so quietly, "Do you know about the secret?" She shared many stories of how the secret shows up in her life and how through the Law of Attraction we live healthy lives. Their life is empowered with Gratitude and blessings are given as though everything has happened and this is how they live each and every day. Blessings they give from the ground they walk on to the boat they fish with; and once the fish is caught, more blessings are sent out to the universe — with every action gratitude is expressed. She sparked my interest from the whisper about the secret. I read the book, now with an urgency I went from store to store until I found the book and CD set. I listened to the CD set over and over again, wherever I drove, the louder the better to block out any other noise. The secret is not really a secret, it is a way of life, a plan of simply living from Love.

Daily Teachings

 "You can do anything you want but you must follow the principals of Law. Eliminate all doubt and replace it with full expectation that you will receive what you are asking for. If you are not receiving what you are asking for, then it is not the law that has failed. It means your doubt is greater than your faith."

~ THE SECRET

How Life Can Happen For Us

The secret of simple living has always been underneath the layers of ages gone by. Each day there are new lessons and blessings. It is through our thoughts and intentional living that we create our existence. Our greatest method of understanding and living with purpose is to ask ourselves if we are thinking in loving ways. I do!

The "Secret" was the start to how life can happen for me and I followed each lead as it came up; studying and learning, to understand what resonates best for my spirit and soul. I'm hooked on filling my needs and desires with the long lost secret within my being. The daily practice of Love and enlightenment from mediation and doing away with all that no longer serves me lifts me higher. It is from this place of peace that I desire to share how beautiful life happens for us through the Law of Attraction, Love for the divine source and universe. Infinite gratitude!

Now with this new vision I was excited and I started looking for a community of likeminded people so I could stay high on life. I never found the community and I fell back into the old patterns, but with each attempt I soon realized what I needed was to know who I was first. Life is not a race, nor is it something we get. Life happens for us as we vibrationally attract things into our Life.

First of all I am God's child, secondly I am one with all that exists on earth. All life started with a seed — it grows and matures, flowers and produces in order to reproduce. This is life simply put, not complicated. In production sharing happens, exchanges in vibration influence the flow of nature. There are certain types of plants and trees that lose their leaves or foliage, this process takes place to protect its source, the trunk and roots, so it can reproduce and give back to its surroundings. This is how humans are meant to live with compassion, gratitude and Love, being simple without expectation.

We have the ability to choose good, live with gratitude, follow the path of many a year, planned by your heart and soul. We get to choose what we think, who we talk to and how we feel. When we choose compassion, forgiveness, surrender and letting go, we are creating a life filled with Love. Allow every uprising to go through you and accept it as a lesson. We are students of life and through our learning we become teachers and guides for the generations to come. May you be the spark, the guiding light for those generations and Love your way Home.

 "Whatever you hold in your mind
on a consistent basis is exactly what
you will experience in your life."

~ ANTHONY ROBBINS

My heart is filled with so much Love for everyone who has touched my Life. I have so much gratitude for all my family — my immediate family, daughter Nicole Penn, son Sean O'Oshea, grandchildren, Kevin Race, Christinna & Hailee Matsuba, and Braydon O'Shea. The Penn Family has grown with me and helped shape the life I live today, Thank you all for being part of my life path. To my life partner Brad you give strength and build me up and support us with so much more than Love.

In light of this most amazing opportunity I thank Brad Simkins for sharing the V.I.P invite and thank him for believing in me. To Lisa Hardwick at Visionary Insight Press, thank you for seeing me with your heart; without your vision we would just be dreaming. Last but not least, Chelle who pulled it all together, blessings to you, you are a beautiful star of light. Namasté

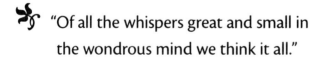 "Of all the whispers great and small in
the wondrous mind we think it all."

~ BRENDA PENN

Your time is limited, don't waste
it living someone else's life. Don't
be trapped by dogma, which is
living the result of other people's
thinking. Don't let the noise of other's
opinion drown your own inner
voice. Everything else is secondary.

~ STEVE JOBS

Barbara McKay

BARBARA MCKAY lives a quiet life, she meditates, does yoga, is forever a student of the mind and still to this day she knows the best blessings in her life are her three beautiful sisters, her three amazing children and her three precious little angels who call her 'Grandma." It took every blessed moment of her life to discover her favorite words are "I Love You, Grandma!"

🌿 Avesha Awakens

I once believed God judged me unworthy,
I once believed in Death,
I once believed medicine could heal me,
I once believed I was constantly in danger of the unknown,
I once believed I was unlovable and broken
Because ...
I once believed what society reflected back to me,
But now ...
The Power of the truth of who I am has awakened,
I love knowing who I am,
I love knowing I am a Divine expression of God,
I love knowing God is my source,
I love knowing I am eternal,
I love knowing that, now, that I have accepted the divinity of who I am
I am free from ... fear, lack and limitation

Today, I am valued for my presence and, as I look out upon the world, I can see the perfection of the contrast provided. I appreciate all the players in this production of my soul. I see the perfection in the deconstruction of my ego, thus allowing the light of my soul to shine forth ... even if it wasn't always so.

When I look back at the woman I once was, I can hardly see myself within the memory. My life began being born to a woman who was emotionally abused and, as much as she tried to do her best, I was always filled with the feeling I was replacing another. This feeling followed me into adulthood, driving me to continuously strive to be something other than who I was. At the same time I turned to alcohol like my momma to numb the pain. It was when I turned 40 that I realized I was messed up. I was married to a man who I became completely dependent upon and, bless his heart, we had one heck of a love-hate relationship that spiraled us into drugs, alcohol and gambling addictions. Our children were given everything except our undivided time and attention. I knew it was time to change when, after another drunken drug-induced argument, I found myself in a hotel room committed to ending my life. I honestly believed my children would be better off, and when I called my then husband he confirmed my beliefs and told me, the world would be better off without me.

This is where God entered my life because I did take the pills and I did cross over. I remember moving into a state of consciousness that permeated my entire being. I was experiencing a love-beauty moment which I had never experienced before, not even as I gave birth did I feel such a love and appreciation for who I am. I remember having a mind connection with God and was told my mission was not yet complete. I was given a choice … I was to choose between returning to my previous body or being re-born as a new baby. I chose to return to my body with the promise from God this was my time. I then found myself floating up over my body and watching as the paramedics entered my room. The female paramedic began to resuscitate me while the male paramedic confirmed there were suicide letters left on the dresser. I remember hearing the female paramedics voice whispering to me, "I am not letting you go." I was then sucked back into my body and as I took my first breathe I exhaled, "you bitch," for I didn't want to leave that divine energy that had filled all my painful memories.

The following few months were confusing, as I had no 3-D vision. Everything I saw was like a projection onto a flat screen. My memories had been temporarily erased, yet I had a knowing within that I was an angel — not of this world. I was drawn to the sun and I floated through my life as if I was only an observer. I had no energetic connection to anything or anybody. My family had become foreign to me. I felt no fear, no separation from the divine essence that had permeated my being during my death experience. I felt as if I was a visitor from another time. My visions of a city were that of mud-huts and I remember looking at everything surrounding me and thinking, look at how far we've come. I was drawn to exchanging my energy with the plants for nourishment and I was mesmerized by the reflection of the light upon everything I saw.

This lasted for a few months and as I look back, it is probably the reason I remained sane, as my then marriage of 22 years began to fall apart. Eventually, the memories returned and the healing of everything I had become and experienced began. I know I was led and guided every step of the way. Over time, I released my need to drink and do drugs. I began nourishing my body with organic foods. I became a ferocious reader. I started counseling and found a spiritual community who loved and accepted me for who I was, opening me up to a whole new world.

Seven years later, I am happily independent. I work part-time for an investor/corporate accountant. I am in the Spiritual practitioner program with full intentions of becoming a minister within The Center of Spiritual Living and I've recently begun assisting our Reverend in facilitating the Foundations class. I am so very thankful I am still alive and able to share my story with you. My journey of awakening began with death, yet my life has become the most joyous, loving experience because of it. I no longer fear death, nor do I fear life. I've traveled many times to many places knowing I am safe. I've discovered my ability to co-create my life with God. I have accepted the divine knowing that God is ALWAYS working in, as and through me.

If you are in a space of sadness or despair, please know with me, God loves you more than life itself — for you are life itself. Find me … join me at any Center of Spiritual Living for I now know at the core of who I am is God, and just as this is true for me, this is also your truth and when two minds join in union anything is possible. I love you!

Special Note: I read in the Wisdom of the Ancients by T.Lobsang Rampa, that, Avesha represents the transition I experienced over a seven-year span. It was an instant 'knowing' then that I would use the pen name, Avesha, when I share my story.

Dedicated to my sisters.

I am eternally grateful to the Center for Spiritual Living in Edmonton, Canada. Please send all proceeds in the form of a donation in my name to the Center for Spiritual Living Edmonton. Link: http://www.centreforspirit.com/

~ Barbara McKay

Hellen Romphf

HELLEN ROMPHF is a Lover of Life, world travelling enthusiast, Mother and Grandmother. She resides in Beautiful British Columbia, Canada, with both daughter and granddaughter close by her side and enjoys the constant change and adventure of everyday life!

❧ The 29th Chapter

A t "chapter 29 years of age" … I had troubles digesting the Zen proverb, "Chop wood, carry water".

I believe my soul arrived hungry on this whirling, swirling, blue abyss and my innate character has always been that of a happy, positive nature, knowing that good would always come my way.

Because of this nature, over the years I have been blessed with offers of good paying jobs and some beautiful relationships.

All of which I had either sabotaged, or realized I had made an inappropriate choice for where my soul needed to be, and I quickly and determinedly let go of people, places and things without a second thought or a backwards glance. And in an ox-like fashion I would push my way through to the next chapter.

Until finally at the age of 29, I hit a wall. And that wall was me.

At that time, I gained a young, trusted female counsellor who, in one of our sessions said to me, "You must be exhausted" and with much exuberance I exclaimed, "Yes!" Yes, I am exhausted she must understand me! She gets it!! What a relief!! She knows how hard my life has been.

And then she said to me, "playing God is a big roll". And it hit me like a brick … I was trying to control all aspects of my life including people, places, things, and not to mention, my child. I figured if I kept my child in good control, my life would be easier. How exhausting for sure!!

We two went on to discover, over the course of time, that I was resisting, resisting my single-parenting responsibilities and that fear was at the helm, driving my life into the ground, causing me to run here and run there like a whirling dervish. Divert this and that, take the easy path — which always inevitably was the hardest path.

Fear, smear, hear, gear, blah, blah, blah. If you have lived in fear, you know what I'm talking about.

And although I had worked two jobs, went to college and found a great job within the government, my daughter was always well-fed, well-clothes and had a warm comfortable roof over her head... we, my counsellor and I, had the epiphany that I was resisting, I was in conflict and incongruent.

Then she handed me "the book," by Louise Hay, *You Can Heal You Life!* and exclaimed that I was to read each of the chapters and do the homework.

When you turn the corner and the soles of your feet feel like you've just had an amazing massage, you know you're on the right path and my resistance was gone. I accepted what was and my life very quickly took many fascinating turns. What a gift women are to one another when we put ourselves aside, open our minds and heads to share our wisdom with one another and accept changes within ourselves!

Some lessons I've learned in life are:

1. Always keep a bag packed and ready for adventure.
2. Avoid the naysayers and let them nay their own way, unless you see a resonated longing in their eyes that beckons you to open your heartstrings and gently play them a melody.
3. Simply reward yourself often, without a glimpse of guilt... eat chocolate.
4. Make faces at small children and buy nice linen.
5. Oh yes, and always pack a blowdryer when you're in Alberta.

Not all lessons need be monumental.

My next greatest gift came from a family member…I considered him my oak tree, my mentor and my confidante. We were to meet and have coffee in a Tim Horton's restaurant just down the hill from where I lived. He said he had something for me, and once we settled within our chairs with our coffee, his eyes lit up and I became very curious.

He said, "What is wrong with this moment?" I began looking around, asking myself internal questions, and I could come up with nothing wrong. Then he pulled something out of his duffle bag. It was a book inside a Glad freezer bag, and he said, "Exactly, there is nothing wrong with this moment," and handed me the book, *The Power Of Now* by Eckhart Tolle.

Once again, I was ready and devoured this book with all the voraciousness of Ants. While devouring, I experienced tingling sensations in my body, my mind exploded as the words jumped off the page and I felt beautiful emotional moments that left my body feeling rejuvenated and safe in the knowing that the only time is NOW. Here it is, a simplified book written to be understood by all.

By the time I finished this book my days were like walking on clouds. I would drive on a sunny day to work and look at the mountains surrounding me and would literally have tears of joy that would run down my face in gratitude of all that is.

People actually said to me for the first time, "I can see your aura," and that "there was the presence of light around me when I walked in a room." I was astounded, floating and utterly delighted with this newfound mindset of NOW. So simple.

"Imagine the Earth devoid of human life, inhabited only by plants and animals. Would it still have a past and a future? Could we still speak of time in any meaningful way? The question "What time is it?" or "What's the date today?" — if anybody were there to ask it — would be quite meaningless. The oak tree or the eagle would be bemused by such a question. "What time?" they would ask. "Well, of course, it's now. The time is now. What else is there?"

~ QUOTE FROM THE POWER OF NOW

I purchased the book over and over again and gave it to anyone and everyone who showed a sparkle of interest. I had to share this! If it made a difference in even one person's life, like it did in mine, I would be ever so grateful.

I still have all the bumps and grinds of daily life, however. Today at 53 manmade calendar years, I have gained a much more intimate relationship with myself and I understand that happiness is not the absence of problems, moreover it's the ability to deal with them. I am the watcher. I stay as conscious as I can with my busy life. There are still so many things I aspire to be and do. But the most important of these things is to remain true to myself: Authentic. To give and receive love openly. Be kind to all I meet and compassionate to those whom are searching. To never be anybody's doormat and say the word "no" with ease and comfort. To remember to take time, if only for a moment, to meditate, reflect, just breathe and remember to take the mental garbage out.

These days, I revel in my time alone and spend as many joyous hours as I can with my granddaughter and daughter, who is my dearest friend. I plan healthy meals and amazing smoothies packed with the goodness of vital health optimizing ingredients. I spend time with a few close friends I call dear and I remember to recall the things I am grateful before bed and upon wakening. I am consciously aware of the things I allow in my personal mind space and allow only those who are uplifting and true in my personal physical space.

Whatever choices we make, we are here to have a joyous experience! If we make a choice and it turns out to be the wrong choice for us, we can make another choice which resonates more closely with our highest vibration.

Dedicated to my daughter Meggan whose very light saved my soul and granddaughter Olivia whose essence of love fills my aura.

At this time I would like to say a special thanks to my mother for the courage she showed and for the life lessons she bestowed upon me. With much love and respect always.

Special thanks to the awakened spiritual wisdom of writers Louise Hay and Eckhart Tolle whose words have helped to enlighten my path…Most humble Blessing!

~ Hellen Romphf

The more and more each is
impelled by that which is intuitive,
or the relying upon the soul force
within, the greater, the farther,
the deeper, the broader, the more
constructive may be the result.

~ EDGAR CAYCE

Angela Serna

ANGELA SERNA *is an Author, Professional Life Coach, Workshop Leader, Seminar Facilitator and Yoga Instructor.* Her passion is helping others create change in their lives through life coaching, workshops, and Yoga. She helps individuals to uncover the mindset that limits success in their relationships, career, health and prosperity. Using simple yet powerful techniques, she guides people toward a realization of their own power, inner wisdom and strengths. She also teaches Stress Management in the Workplace and has an enormous passion for the Conscious Parenting Workshops that she leads.

Angela@AngelaSerna.com
AngelaSerna.com

Listening To The Heart

L istening to the heart when it whispers — Rumi says, when you wake up early in the morning don't go back to sleep, listen, "the breeze at dawn has secrets to tell you." This is when the world is the quietest and I so believe this is when I have the most clarity. If its answers that I'm searching for, just granting the mind a chance to get quiet, brings clarity and solutions.

I've received some fantastic ideas to incorporate into my workshops at 4:00 a.m. in the morning. If I awake at three or four in the morning for no reason, I just allow my mind to become quiet, by being still and listening. This is also what meditation does for me. Meditation is my direct connection to source, it's a time when I am not doing the talking... I'm listening and the answers come, I am just being. My day goes so much smoother, things fall into place where I may have struggled otherwise. By allowing my mind to get quiet and asking for guidance before any of the workshops that I lead or Yoga classes that I teach, it's amazing how I'm guided through the class, it just flows. I also ask for guidance not only for myself to help bring benefits to those attending my class, but I also ask for guidance for my students to be able to receive the benefits. There have been days when I've walked into teach a Yoga class when I've been going through some pain of my own and not really feeling worthy to teach others and wondering what I could possibly offer them today. This is what the mind will do if I permit it to do so, if I am not aware. By having that awareness and taking the time to center myself, focusing in on the heart center, listening, and asking for simple guidance, it's amazing how life will flow. This is what connecting to source, your higher power, The Universe or God, whatever you choose to call it, does when you connect to it. It frees you to go to that place within and listen to your heart. When I am centered, without fail, I always have students after class say, "You always seem to know just exactly what I need" or "That was an amazing class." My thoughts are the Universe always knows exactly what you need, I just open myself up to the guidance.

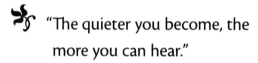 "The quieter you become, the
more you can hear."

~ RAM DASS

Letting Go of Expectations

So much pain and suffering is caused because of our expectations for other people to behave in a certain way or in the manner that we think they should behave in. It's not someone else's job to make us happy, it's our job, and letting go of expectations which we put on others is definitely a step in the right direction to discover happiness. Happiness is an inside job, but you have to do the work. At times, the work is as simple as connecting to your higher self, freeing the mind to get quiet as you connect to that power within you, realizing just how amazing you are, and having the inner knowing that you are capable of accomplishing great things. But, you have to believe in yourself, no one can do this for you.

Most relationships are full of expectations. We often expect others to do, be and act like we, ourselves, would in most situations. We must realize that the stress we put on others when we have these expectations, and it is also stress that we are creating for ourselves by becoming frustrated when people don't live up to our expectations. It doesn't matter how fleeting the expectation, expectation sets us up for disappointment every time. Just because I would act in a certain manner does not mean everyone else should be acting, reacting, and responding in that same manner.

By nature it all comes back to wanting to be loved and accepted. It's always so interesting to me when I've observed those around me be dependent on others for love and acceptance. Their happiness depends on this and, by nature, our self-worth is dependent on this also. I watch as I see an individual who thinks they are losing their best friend of many years because their friend's spouse is controlling and manipulating. I can see the devastation as he feels like he has lost a longtime friend. Once they iron a few things out and matters appear to be back to normal, I notice the relief, the happiness, and the excitement. I have also observed an acquaintance who dates a guy who has never treated her the way she or any women deserves to be treated. But in the moments when he decides to embrace her fully and he is treating her kindly, her whole world changes — even if it's just for moments, even though the bad is far worse than the good, her happiness depends on those few moments. Then it all falls away. When he is not fully embracing her, she is longing for the happiness of when he is, and holding on to the hope that he will change. I have also watched someone completely lose themselves while just trying to fit into another person's world, precisely because we depend on a significant other to make us happy. Instead, we need to allow ourselves to live our truth and trust the process of life, for what is meant to be will be.

I think how sad it is that, as a society, we are so dependent on others to make us happy. This is all lack of self-love which is the result of low self-esteem. If we had confidence within us, YES we would be affected by all of these happenings and feel the hurt feelings, but they would not take over our whole world. If we truly loved ourselves, we would not be so dependent on others for our happiness. If we truly loved ourselves these people would automatically be drawn to us, because happy people are attractive people. The pressure and expectations which we put on others is irrational, all for our own happiness. The happiness that we are looking for outside of ourselves, can only be found within.

Initially, watching this in so many relationships beyond significant others, I then looked at myself and saw how my expectations of my mom have destroyed my own happiness and inner peace. Even as a grown adult, when I know that all I want is to feel like she cares and have her support when I am going through a tough time in my life, I'm now clear she is incapable of doing that from where she is right now. How the atmosphere changed since my dad made his transition, how her choices have appeared outrageous and extremely shocking to me. But these are my judgments and my expectations — they are mine, not hers. I've heard people talk about how they have never had a fulfilling relationship with their mom, and there was a point in time when I could not imagine not have a relationship with my mom. I have often thought which is worse, to have never had a wonderful relationship with your mom or to have had it and to have lost it. I think the latter, because if I had never had it I would have no expectations of her behaving in a certain way, a way that I know she was once capable of. She is now incapable of this from where she is in life, although I may still long for it. I knew she was in the midst of her own pain, and when we are in pain, we sometimes project that onto others; this didn't make it any easier, as I was also still grieving the loss of my dad.

But how could she do this to me? DAILY for months after my dad's passing, I would call each morning to talk to her on my commute to class; most every afternoon I called to check on her and would often talk for an hour, and on a nightly basis after I put my son to bed, I would always spend at least an hour, sometimes two, on the phone with her. She lives four hours away, so in addition to the time on the phone, I made trips home when I could. I knew she was feeling alone and in pain, so anything I could do to lessen it I did.

After months of this it was suddenly like she turned into a different person. Her relationship with me had no importance, none whatsoever. How could this be? Not only was our relationship now insignificant to her, it was like she felt the need to punish me on top of it. I spent well over a year trying to reason with her, trying to make sense of it with painful conversations and endless emails that led nowhere. I let it consume me. I still don't have the answers, but I knew I had one of two choices — I could stay in this state of negativity, granting it permission to rule my world, or I could make a choice to take care of me and heal myself. When I made that decision things lined up for me in perfect divine order. I had to learn to trust the journey, even when I didn't understand it.

It was easy for her to choose me as the object of her anger and frustration, because I was the only one who stepped outside of her box of rules, her limitations, her fear, her control, and the standards of her society. The criticism of me doing anything a little bit different than how it had always been done, and the judgments of any imperfections that she saw in my life, were circumstances I could no longer let control me. I knew I had to go find that place within me where happiness lives. Where freedom is! I had to find my truth, my path, and just because my path is different from hers doesn't make it wrong. All the criticism I've received, the hurtful words that have been said, the judgments which have been made, and the love that was now conditional, were disappointing and painful — but it was all well worth it!

Mom, you were my foundation for life, my rock and now suddenly you are not. This, however, was my lesson, my lesson to practice gratitude in the core of chaos and pain, a lesson to work through my codependent issues which came from my childhood. It is only my hope that one day you are able to love me for who I am and not for who you want me to be. I forgive you because had I not had this experience I would not be the person I am today, living my truth. I am grateful. It is necessary to forgive to be able to move forward in life. Forgiving doesn't mean that we condone the behavior of others, we forgive them to free ourselves.

Growth is painful, change is painful, but nothing is as painful as staying stuck where you don't belong.

 "Pain is inevitable, suffering is optional."

~ BUDDHA

The Healing Process

Maybe, now and then, it's not whispers of the heart...sometimes it could be that Voice inside of us speaking loud and clear. Then again maybe that voice had to speak loud and clear for me to finally be able to hear it and I am grateful for the volume. When we are in pain or feeling disappointed, that seems to be when it's the hardest to focus in order to encourage the mind to become quiet. This is when you just have to surrender to all the chaos that is going on around you, and go to a place of gratitude where you know there is a lesson waiting for you. My affirmation: "Thank you for the lesson that I know is in this for me." "I know that all is working for my higher good." You just have to trust the process of life. Let it go — letting it go sounds so simple, but when you are in the midst of pain it can be one of the hardest things to do.

Going to that place of gratitude, healing the child within me was huge, because it's the inner child inside me who is being disappointed and feeling angry, not the intellectual person who I have grown into. Healing my inner child made me realize that these expectations were not serving me, they were only keeping me stuck in this state of negativity. Once I let them go, I had this voice inside of me which spoke loud and clear, "You do not need her approval, you don't need anyone's approval, you can do this on your own. She is never going to be the person that you want her to be and she is never going to support the person that you have grown into; but you've got this, you can move forward in life and be the person that you were sent here to be. Let it all go." This was considerably more than a whisper from the heart — I've never heard a voice so loud and so clear! It was literally like I woke up, I got it. Once we give up our false self (the ego which helps us justify the hurt, resentment, and disappointment), then we can hear spirit speak to us. I am grateful for that loud voice that spoke so clearly. It was like I was instantly injected with this sense of self confidence that I had never felt before.

Healing the Inner Child

When I realized that it was my inner child who was responding and reacting to everything taking place around this issue with my mom, I knew what I needed to do. I needed to heal what was inside me that continued to feel hurt, angry and disappointed — that inner child within me who had been carrying around wounds and discouragement from my early years. These situations are varied for everyone — it could be seemingly unimportant events that took place when we were growing up — it doesn't have to be anything one would consider a traumatic experience.

However, when we take a look at the emotions or beliefs which were instilled in us from childhood, whether its fear, anger, disappointment, feeling unworthy, not being good enough, etc., this is what affects our reactions to experiences as we grow into adults. All adults are a product of their childhood! Even those of us who think that we had a good upbringing. If we haven't taken the time to do the inner work, there are beliefs and perceptions which are limiting us today from being the person we are meant to be. Don't get me wrong, our parents were doing the absolute best they knew how with the knowledge, consciousness and understanding that they had at the time. There is no one to blame and there are no justified resentments.

As much as I knew on an intellectual level, that I do not need to depend on anyone else for my own inner happiness, I was still allowing myself to be affected by my mom's behavior. It was the small child in me who continued to feel hurt, disappointed and betrayed. It was that little girl within me who was responding and reacting to all that was taking place. I have now learned that I have the ability to embrace my own inner child. Speak to the small child within you, take yourself back to any childhood memories or stages of your youth and embrace that young child and send it love, comfort and support that maybe it never got while you were growing up. You are the only person today who can nurture and support that precious child within you; embrace all parts of it. Every adult is a result of their childhood emotions which stay stored within them if they are not nurtured, healed or released. When you feel like your pain is being caused by someone else's action, know that when you heal areas which need to be healed within yourself, the pain will no longer show up in this manner. Once in a while, we have to experience the darkness before we can appreciate the light.

Loving yourself is key to healing and creating self-confidence. With self-confidence you have freedom. When we love and approve of ourselves exactly as we are; it's when we are not dependent on others for happiness, we will find it within ourselves. Confident people can do anything and sometimes you have to do what is best for you, which is nothing more than simple self-care. I let go of my expectations that others would grow as I have grown. How could they, when they didn't have my life experiences, since it was those experiences that have led me to the inner work I have done. My advice for anyone wanting to move through any painful situations which life has offered them, is to take the opportunity to do the inner work, spend time in stillness, forgive and take several moments to heal your inner child. Affirmations, gratitude, meditation, forgiveness, and healing your inner child have brought me happiness, freedom, and peace of mind, and this is when you, too, can hear the whispers of the heart. This is where you can open your heart and love from that place of pure unconditional love. Embrace all obstacles and challenges — they are just an opportunity to grow.

 "Accept — then act. Whatever the present moment contains, accept it as if you had chosen it. Always work with it, not against it. Make it your friend and ally, not your enemy. This will miraculously transform your whole life."

~ ECKHART TOLLE

Meditation for Loving Yourself and Loving All Beings

As you sit in meditation bring your focus and attention to your breath to help quiet the mind and become centered. After several breaths, bring your attention and awareness to your heart center and imagine the doors of the heart opening wide and as Louise Hay says it so beautifully, "know that there is an infinite well of love deep inside of you." Breathe that pure unconditional love into every cell of your body. With each deep breath, feel that love flowing through all the fibers of your being. Affirm: I Love and accept myself just as I am. I am Perfect exactly as I am. Is there any part of your body which you feel isn't fully serving you? Send extra pure unconditional love to that part of your body. We can heal what we love and accept, and what we resist persists.

Now that you are swimming in this sea of pure unconditional love, imagine someone very dear to you; as you picture that person, surround them with pure unconditional love and watch them as they radiate that love to everyone around them. As you continue to breathe, inhale love, exhale, transmitting that love out. Imagine another person who is neutral to you, you may not know them very well, it could be a neighbor, co-worker, or someone who has waited on you at the grocery store and send them heartfelt love. Inhale love and exhale, sending it out, watch them as they shower that love on those around them. Now imagine that person who brings stress into your world, someone who may irritate or frustrate you, maybe it's someone who has wronged you, send them that heartfelt pure unconditional love. As you surround them with this love, watch them as they allow that love to overflow to those around them, and imagine them returning love back to you — feel what that feels like, breathe it in. Now, extend that love to your friends and family, throughout your entire community. Now, take that love and allow it to expand throughout your city, your state, the surrounding states, as you send that love throughout the United States and watch it flow into other countries, as you send it throughout the entire universe.

Choose a place on the planet where you feel additional healing is needed and surround that area with love, see people happy and well-fed. Or you may know someone who is in need of an extra bit of love, light, and healing energy, surround them with all that you have within you, send it out.

If you are looking to shift your energy, silently send love to every single person you encounter throughout your day, strangers, family members, co-workers, neighbors — and especially send it to those who irritate you, frustrate you or bring stress into your world, surround them with love!

New Beginnings are often described as painful endings, and nothing ever goes away until it teaches us what we need to know.

Dedicated to Jacqueline Steinbeck, EPT Practitioner, your work has helped me through some of life's most challenging times. The growth which has come from working with you has benefited my life immensely and I am grateful.

To two very special people, Heather Dennison and Renee Radcliff, you have been of immense support through some of the greatest times of my life, as well as through some of the most difficult times. I am forever grateful for our friendship of many years. The support that you have shown is deeply appreciated and I look forward to the many years to come.

~ Angela Serna

Chelle Thompson

CHELLE THOMPSON is Editor-Publisher of Inspiration Line, and has an extensive background in recovery programs, motivational counseling, psychology and theology. Inspiration Line's Meaningful Life website and global e-magazine reach more than 235 countries worldwide. Chelle's skills in international travel writing and human relations provide this project with an insightful and diversified foundation. In 1991, Chelle left a successful advertising career in Southern California and followed her Inner Voice to New Mexico, where she knew no one. In Santa Fe, she established a holistic center and published a monthly magazine that was distributed nationally.

Bringing Enlightenment Down to Earth

An interesting thing about humans is that when we find something that brings us joy, we often want to stay deeply immersed and never let go. This even applies to our spiritual pursuits. When we recognize and embrace the Whispers of the Heart that bring Inner Guidance, our life is changed forever. Like John Denver's "Rocky Mountain High," we find soaring with Spirit more gratifying than anything else we've known.

Many folks love the thrill of rides at Disneyland because they whisk us away from our day-to-day realities. However, if we all became amusement park junkies, would we EVER discover why we're here on this planet? We might think we're getting a "clearer" picture high atop the Matterhorn. Aren't we closer to the Heavens up there? Or are we simply choosing another form of escape?

Eventually, the time comes for each of us to get back down to basics and deal with our human issues, problems and challenges — the "stuff" that shapes our character and charts our destinies.

If we are looking for an "easy out" rather than ways to elevate ourselves and be fully present, we can flee into the ethers and avoid life whenever the going gets tough. Sometimes the magical qualities of expanded-growth experiences have an almost narcotic effect … I think of it as The Drama of Phenomena … and it often appears to be the long-awaited solution we've been craving.

Incredible insights can certainly be gained from a multitude of extraordinary practitioners, counselors, clergy, shaman and motivators through individual/group therapy, classes, seminars, and other guidance sessions.

But, will we choose people to work with who are dedicated to our empowerment, or those who simply operate as middle men, keeping themselves or their philosophy as the "required link" between us and Source? More critical, will we use even the purest arenas as our drugs of choice — trying to elude reality by "rising above it all"?

Why are we alive? I believe it's to bring GOD/SOURCE ENERGY INTO FORM here on Earth. Not merely to pop in when everything feels wonderful, then hide out in various modalities when adversities arise. Following is a related poem that I wrote several years ago entitled:

"DETOURS"

Sometimes we experience slight dimensional snags...
Like catching your sleeve
On an unforeseen splinter
As you move through the passageway.

The journey's the goal, our path is the point...
But the luxury of lesson,
Each excursion into mirrors,
Enlightens us along the passageway.

Detours cause us pain, changes filled with turmoil...
Thereby evoking QUESTIONS,
As precious stepping stones,
To guide us down the passageway.

Looking back at our detours, we catch the reflection...
They made us who we are,
And awakened our
Reason for Being, in the passageway.

I woke up with that first verse in the middle of the night and quickly wrote it down so it wouldn't be lost in my dreams when morning came — later it blossomed into a whole poem. To me, it means that as we're going through life, we sometimes get "snagged" into situations that are not for our highest good...like "splinters."

It's important that we stay conscious in our journey and find the "stepping stones" that are essential for us to evolve, rather than to go on blindly repeating old patterns.

If we will look into the "mirrors" (insights) from each "lesson" we are taught, we'll discover that they are actually valuable treasures in the "Passageway" that is Life.

"Detours" (abusive environments, painful relationships, etc.) are the routes we take when snagged. As we awaken, however, we begin to ASK QUESTIONS of ourselves, like: "How did I let this happen?" "Why did I choose to be there or to do that?"

The bottom line is that THERE ARE NO ANSWERS UNTIL THERE ARE QUESTIONS. When we contemplate our so-called "mistakes," we see that they reflect important information back to us...thereby developing our essence and moving us toward our ultimate potential.

Dedicated to my dear husband, Bruce — my best friend and support system — your love empowers and fills me with joy each and every day.

I am thankful for being born a naturally-open vessel who is able to receive (and now follow) ethereal guidance … in my head, on billboards and radio, in randomly-selected book passages and from friends who, later, couldn't recall saying the messages I needed to hear. I'm specifically grateful for the teachings of Ernest Holmes, Hermes Trismegistus, Emmet Fox, Dr. Toni Grant, Dr. David Viscott, Susan Jeffers, A Course in Miracles, and the Grand Spirit Dr. James Peebles. Thank you Lisa Hardwick, my publisher and friend, for reawakening my passion for writing.

~ Chelle Thompson

I feel there are two people inside
me — me and my intuition. If I
go along against her, she'll screw
me every time, and if I follow
her, we get along quite nicely.

~ KIM BASINGER

Lisa Hardwick

LISA HARDWICK is a publishing project director, author, speaker, workshop leader and a board member for her local chapter Children's Advocacy Center in East Central Illinois.

She resides in Charleston, Illinois, where she enjoys spending time with her family and her whimsically-fun friends. She also enjoys traveling throughout the country, facilitating writing workshops and assisting others with sharing their inspirational stories through written form.

To connect with Lisa visit www.lisahardwick.com

Following the
❧ Divine Whisper

"If given the chance, what is the most important piece of advice you would share with your younger self?" This question was sent to me in a recent email, and upon reading it, I immediately knew my answer: Trust your intuition.

Do you honor that whisper you hear that speaks to you from deep within your being? Some call it the *whisper of the divine*, others call it *trusting your gut* or you may have simply heard it named *intuition*. No matter what you choose to call it, I believe once you develop the ability to notice it and allow it to guide your thoughts and actions, your life will take on an entirely new light.

I have an incredible relationship with the *divine voice* that speaks to me. When I was younger, I would *hear* it quite often, yet I never told anyone because I thought it was something to be ashamed of. It wasn't until many years later that I realized I have been extremely intuitive from a very young age, and having these abilities was actually a gift and not something to be distressed about. Once I found others who also had this *awareness*, it brought a whole new meaning to my life. This is when I chose to learn about the different ways to hear *the voice* more clearly and more often.

With practice I became more aware of *the voice*. I would be so happy and feel so much more balanced in my life when it would show up that I wanted to be connected with it as often as possible. I learned to do this through different methods of meditation and later taught others how to meditate utilizing guided imagery, creative visualization and other techniques. I would present these tools at workshops I was invited to participate in throughout the year.

If you are reading this and still aren't sure if you've heard the divine whisper of your heart, perhaps you simply aren't aware of it when it shows up. I will share with you one of my typical days as an example of how I tune in to the divine whisper — with the intention to assist you in better understanding how to be aware when it happens to you. Because it *does* happen to you each and every day.

My afternoon was really incredible that day. I had to go to the Superstore. You know, those stores that have everything from baked goods to tires. We have *two* Superstores that I can choose to visit; one is across our small university town and the other is approximately 10 miles away. As I approached the traffic light I felt the urge to go to the store that was 10 miles away (versus 1.5 miles away) and I kept thinking to myself, "Why am I feeling this way? It's a bit ridiculous to go all that way! Oh well, if I still feel the urge when the light turns green, then I will make a right turn and go to the store farthest away." So the light turned green, I turned right, and drove to the far away store.

Once in the store I began noticing it was taking much longer than usual to find all the items on my list. I did find the items I was looking for, but it took forever! I am usually a very fast shopper, yet when I would look at my list I would think, "Oh nooooo — that item is all the way on the other side of the store ... again!" Needless to say, I was getting my exercise and blowing up my FitBit!

As I was in the checkout line, I reminded myself that I was right where I was supposed to be. If the shopping took longer than expected, that is okay because it's all divine timing and everything was working out for my highest good.

I checked out and bundled up to go out to my car. It's freezing here and the wind is fierce during this time of year. I made it to my car and started putting my things in the back, when I looked up and saw a small gray-haired woman trying to navigate her cart in the strong winds, and she looked quite distraught. The only things in her cart were two furnace filters and her purse, which didn't assist with making her cart very weighted or more manageable. Then, we made eye contact, and she gave me a little grin. I grinned back and I yelled out to her, "Did you lose your car? That has happened to *me* before!" She replied "Yes, I've been walking around out here for 20 minutes and I can't find it!"

Oh my goodness... 20 minutes!? She must been *freezing!*

I hurried over and took her cart and grabbed her furnace filters that were being tossed around by the wind as if in a small cage and I said, "Hi, my friend, my name is Lisa and you can trust me. I promise I am a safe person. You can either get in my car and we will drive around and find your car *or* you can tell me what it looks like, the license plate number and you can go inside and get warm and I will drive around and find it *for* you."

Well, she headed straight for the passenger door of my car! She must have decided rather quickly that I was a trustworthy looking person! We drove around very slowly for close to a half hour. We went up and down each aisle and we talked and laughed and then laughed some more. She kept saying, "You're telling me you've lost your car before so I won't feel bad—aren't you!?" And I replied, "Oh, how I wish that was the case!"...and then we laughed even *more*.

And then we found it! Her car was *completely* on the other side of the parking lot. It was almost the last aisle we drove down.

I didn't get her name, but during our conversation I did ask her if she lived in this particular small town...and she said "I sure *do*—I live at 306 Prairie Avenue! I've been there for *years!*"

Well, "Mrs. 306 Prairie Avenue," I am positive I was supposed to meet you today...and I am also grateful I was aware, listened and followed the divine whisper I *heard* this afternoon because it always leads me to exactly where I am supposed to be.

Dedicated to Cole Miller and Maci Miller — because of you, my heart is overflowing.

I have much gratitude for the guidance and wisdom I've been given from the spiritual teachers and mentors I've been so fortunate to be connected to.

~ Lisa Hardwick

🌿 Closing Meditation

Y ou may find this guided script to be a helpful tool in discovering the still, wise and powerful voice within. Consider making a recording of it in your own voice and play it back versus attempting to just read it silently. The power of your own voice is a mighty tool when it comes to accessing the wisdom of your heart. Professionals may also opt to use it as a guide for clients and students as well. Either way, it is my utmost desire that however you choose to utilize it, may you tap into the Great Spring of Consciousness that runs deep within us all.

Optional tools for the journey:

☙ Stones:
- Clear Quartz – Enhances communication
- Rose Quartz – Increases the connection to the heart; Enhances self-love and personal insight

Directions: Hold them in your hand during the meditation or place them nearby to increase your awareness.

☙ Essential Oils:
- Rose – Opens the heart and increases inner vision
- Sandalwood – Increases insightfulness and sensitivity
- Frankincense – Opens the channels to Divine inspiration
- Neroli – Quiets the mind and increases mental clarity

Directions: Apply one to two drops to the palms of your hands and rub briskly. Bring your hands to your face and inhale deeply. You may also add 6-8 drops to your diffuser to create a similar effect.

ᴄᴏ Journal and Pen
Directions: Record your insights.

A Guided Journey to the Answers Within

Let's begin by finding a nice, quiet and comfortable space where you can be alone without any interruptions for several minutes. Find a comfortable position. That may mean lying on your back or easing back into a chair. Whatever you choose, be sure it is a position that you can maintain for the next several moments. Close your eyes and bring your attention to your breath. Follow the gentle rhythm of your belly expanding and contracting as you inhale ... and exhale. Notice the gentle ebb and flow of your abdomen as it expands and contracts. (Pause.)

In a moment, I am going to invite you to inhale deeply to the count of three and exhale to the count of three. (Wait for exhalation.) Inhale ... 1 ... 2 ... 3 ... exhale ... 1 ... 2 ... 3. Again, inhale ... 1 ... 2 ... 3 ... exhale ... 1 ... 2 ... 3. Now once more ... 1 ... 2 ... 3 ... exhale ... 1 ... 2 ... 3. Good.

Continue this pattern ... 1 ... 2 ... 3 ... exhale ... 1 ... 2 ... 3. (Pause for a few more cycles of breath.) On your next inhalation, I'd like to invite you to pause and hold the breath at the top of the inhale for a count of three and then exhale. Inhale ... 1 ... 2 ... 3 ... pause ... 1 ... 2 ... 3 ... exhale ... 1 ... 2 ... 3. Again ... inhale ... 1 ... 2 ... 3 ... pause ... 1 ... 2 ... 3 ... and exhale ... 1 ... 2 ... 3 ... Allow your breath to return back to its natural rhythm. (Pause.)

Now, gently bring your awareness to your chest area. Notice the expanding and contracting as you inhale and exhale. Now, I'd like for you to imagine the bud of a rose sitting right at your heart space.

Notice its color, its texture, its size. (Pause.) Now, imagine this bud opening… slowly … petal by petal … unwinding … expanding outward.

Allow yourself to be completely immersed in its tranquil beauty. (Pause.) Inhale deeply and imagine its pungent aroma entering your nose. Breathe this enchanting fragrance into your lungs and allow yourself to become completely submerged in its intoxicating essence, allowing yourself to become more and more relaxed with each inhalation and exhalation. (Pause.)

Now, think of a question, a problem or situation that you would like more information about, and on your next breath, pull that energy into your heart space. Feel your chest expanding and contracting, as you tap into the Divine wisdom that dwells within. (Pause.)

Become aware of any subtle changes or sensations in your body. Are you experiencing any tightness anywhere? If so, what is the message it brings you? Do you feel warmth or at peace? If so, where is it located? Just observe what is happening within your body. There is no need to judge or struggle. You don't need to figure it out … just observe … (Pause approximately 30 seconds.)

What thoughts, ideas, insights or impressions come to mind? (Pause.) Do you feel a stirring within? Do you feel excited, or perhaps blocked? Just observe what is happening within you right now … (Pause.) Notice if there are any colors or visions that rise in your consciousness … (Pause.) Are there any words or phrases or perhaps even lyrics to a song that come to mind? Just allow yourself to observe … (Pause.) Now, allow your heart space to expand even further as you offer gratitude and appreciation for the wisdom that has come to you during this sacred time. (Pause.)

Gradually … gently … bring your attention back to your breath. Follow the rising and the falling of your belly. (Pause.) Become aware of the floor or chair supporting you below. (Pause.) Become aware of your feet and hands, toes and fingers, and begin to move them in whatever way feels good to you. Stretch out your arms … your legs … giving thanks to your body for being such a wonderful and loving instrument of peace for you today. (Pause.) When you feel ready, you may open your eyes, feeling completely relaxed, rejuvenated and inspired to move forward.

If you feel guided, grab your journal or notebook and jot down any insights or awarenesses that came to you during this meditation. Don't hold back, anything and everything counts. Even if it doesn't make sense to you now, write it down anyway. Its meaning may become clearer to you in the future.

It is important to honor the message or messages that came through to you during this special time. Have faith in your intuition. Take action that will support your spirit. It is with the doing that comes the understanding. We cannot create change by just thinking about it; we must take action in order to create the change we wish to see. Trust the wisdom of your heart. It will never steer you wrong. Know that you can come back to this special place whenever you are in need of guidance, direction or inspiration … at anytime, in any place. From my heart to yours … Namaste`

MARCI CAGEN is a gentle, loving and supportive spiritual coach and teacher with a private practice in Arizona. She has helped many people find their personal mind-body connection and listen to their own inner truth. Marci has a unique ability to transform her own inspirational life story into practical tools and knowledge for others to learn and grow from. Her mission is to empower others to live happy, healthy, and love-filled lives through coaching, workshops and retreats.

For more information, please visit her website: www.MarciCagen.com or email: marci@marcicagen.com.

❧ Resources

The following list of resources are for the national headquarters; search in your yellow pages under "Community Services" for your local resource agencies and support groups.

AIDS

CDC National AIDS Hotline
(800) 342-2437

ALCOHOL ABUSE

Al-Anon Family Group Headquarters
1600 Corporate Landing Parkway
Virginia Beach, VA 23454-5617
(888) 4AL-ANON
www.al-anon.alateen.org

Alcoholics Anonymous (AA)
General Service Office
475 Riverside Dr., 11th Floor
New York, NY 10115
(212) 870-3400
www.alcoholics-anonymous.org

Children of Alcoholics Foundation
164 W. 74th Street
New York, NY 10023
(800) 359-COAF
www.coaf.org

Mothers Against Drunk Driving
MADD
P.O. Box 541688
Dallas, TX 75354
(800) GET-MADD
www.madd.org

National Association of Children of Alcoholics (NACoA)
11426 Rockville Pike, #100
Rockville, MD 20852
(888) 554-2627
www.nacoa.net

Women for Sobriety
P.O. Box 618
Quartertown, PA 18951
(215) 536-8026
www.womenforsobriety.org

CHILDREN'S RESOURCES

Child Molestation

ChildHelp USA/Child Abuse Hotline
15757 N. 78th St.
Scottsdale, AZ 85260
(800) 422-4453
www.childhelpusa.org

Prevent Child Abuse America
200 South Michigan Avenue, 17th Floor
Chicago, IL 60604
(312) 663-3520
www.preventchildabuse.org

Crisis Intervention

Girls and Boys Town National Hotline
(800) 448-3000
www.boystown.org

Children's Advocacy Center of East Central Illinois
(If your heart feels directed to make a donation to this center,
please include Lisa Hardwick's name in the memo)
616 6th Street
Charleston, IL 61920
(217) 345-8250
http://caceci.org

Children of the Night
14530 Sylvan St.
Van Nuys, CA 91411
(800) 551-1300
www.childrenofthenight.org

National Children's Advocacy Center
210 Pratt Avenue
Huntsville, AL 35801
(256) 533-KIDS (5437)
www.nationalcac.org

Co-Dependency

Co-Dependents Anonymous
P.O. Box 33577
Phoenix, AZ 85067
(602) 277-7991
www.codependents.org

Suicide, Death, Grief

AARP Grief and Loss Programs
(800) 424-3410
www.aarp.org/griefandloss

Grief Recovery Institute
P.O. Box 6061-382
Sherman Oaks, CA 91413
(818) 907-9600
www.grief-recovery.com

Suicide Awareness Voices of Education
Minneapolis, MN 55424
(952) 946-7998
Suicide National Hotline
(800) 784-2433

DOMESTIC VIOLENCE

National Coalition Against Domestic Violence
P.O. Box 18749
Denver, CO 80218
(303) 831-9251
www.ncadv.org

National Domestic Violence Hotline
P.O. Box 161810
Austin, TX 78716
(800) 799-SAFE
www.ndvh.org

DRUG ABUSE

Cocaine Anonymous National Referral Line
(800) 347-8998
National Helpline of Phoenix House
(800) COCAINE
www.drughelp.org

National Institute of Drug Abuse
(NIDA)
6001 Executive Blvd., Room 5213,
Bethesda, MD 20892-9561, Parklawn
Building
Info: (301) 443-6245
Help: (800) 662-4357
www.nida.nih.gov

EATING DISORDERS

Overeaters Anonymous
National Office
P.O. Box 44020
Rio Rancho, NM 87174-4020
(505) 891-2664
www.overeatersanonymous.org

GAMBLING

Gamblers Anonymous
International Service Office
P.O. Box 17173
Los Angeles, CA 90017
(213) 386-8789
www.gamblersanonymous.org

HEALTH ISSUES

American Chronic Pain Association
P.O. Box 850
Rocklin, CA 95677
(916) 632-0922
www.theacpa.org

American Holistic Health Association
P.O. Box 17400
Anaheim, CA 92817
(714) 779-6152
www.ahha.org

The Chopra Center at La Costa Resort and Spa Deepak Chopra, M.D.
2013 Costa Del Mar
Carlsbad, CA 92009
(760) 494-1600
www.chopra.com

The Mind-Body Medical Institute
110 Francis St., Ste. 1A
Boston, MA 02215
(617) 632-9530 Ext. 1
www.mbmi.org

National Health Information Center
P.O. Box 1133
Washington, DC 20013-1133
(800) 336-4797
www.health.gov/NHIC

Preventive Medicine Research Institute
Dean Ornish, M.D.
900 Brideway, Ste 2
Sausalito, CA 94965
(415) 332-2525
www.pmri.org

MENTAL HEALTH

American Psychiatric Association of America
1400 K St. NW
Washington, DC 20005
(888) 357-7924
www.psych.org

Anxiety Disorders Association of America
11900 Parklawn Dr., Ste. 100
Rockville, MD 20852
(310) 231-9350
www.adaa.org

The Help Center of the American Psychological Association
(800) 964-2000
www.helping.apa.org

National Center for Post Traumatic Stress Disorder
(802) 296-5132
www.ncptsd.org

National Alliance for the Mentally Ill
2107 Wilson Blvd., Ste. 300
Arlington, VA 22201
(800) 950-6264
www.nami.org

National Depressive and Manic-Depressive Association
730 N. Franklin St., Ste. 501
Chicago, IL 60610
(800) 826-3632
www.ndmda.org

National Institute of Mental Health
6001 Executive Blvd.
Room 81884, MSC 9663
Bethesda, MD 20892
(301) 443-4513
www.nimh.nih.gov

SEX ISSUES

Rape, Abuse and Incest
National Network
(800) 656-4673
www.rainn.org

National Council on Sexual Addiction and Compulsivity
P.O. Box 725544
Atlanta, GA 31139
(770) 541-9912
www.ncsac.org

SMOKING

Nicotine Anonymous World Services
419 Main St., PMB #370
Huntington Beach, CA 92648
(415) 750-0328
www.nicotine-anonymous.org

STRESS ISSUES

The Biofeedback & Psychophysiology Clinic
The Menninger Clinic
P.O. Box 829
Topeka, KS 66601-0829
(800) 351-9058
www.menninger.edu

New York Open Center
83 Spring St.
New York, NY 10012
(212) 219-2527
www.opencenter.org

The Stress Reduction Clinic Center for Mindfulness
University of Massachusetts
Medical Center
55 Lake Ave., North
Worcester, MA 01655
(508) 856-2656

TEEN

Al-Anon/Alateen
1600 Corporate Landing Parkway
Virginia Beach, VA 23454-5617
(888) 425-2666
www.al-anon.alateen.org

Planned Parenthood
810 Seventh Ave.
New York, NY 10019
(800) 230-PLAN
www.plannedparenthood.org

Hotlines for Teenagers
Girls and Boys Town National Hotline
(800) 448-3000

ChildHelp National Child Abuse Hotline
(800) 422-4453

Just for Kids Hotline
(888) 594-KIDS

National Child Abuse Hotline
(800) 792-5200

National Runaway Hotline
(800) 621-4000

National Youth Crisis Hotline
(800)-HIT-HOME

Suicide Prevention Hotline
(800) 827-7571

❧ Bibliography

Andrews, Ted. (2012)
Animal Speak: The Spiritual and Magical Powers of Creatures Great and Small.
Woodbury, MN: Llwellyn Publications.

Beckwith , Michael Bernard.
Life Visioning Process"

Benson, Herbert. (1975).
Relaxation Response.
New York, NY. Harper Torch

Success Principles: How to Get from Where You Are to Where You Want to Be.
New York, NY: Collins
Chopra, Deepak, M.D. (1990.)

Choquette, Sonia.
Answer Is Simple … Love yourself, Live your Spirit
Hay House

Cohen, Alan.
"Create A Masterpiece; When mistakes turn into miracles."
healyourlife.com. N.p., 31 Dec. 2010. Web. 13 Mar. 2011.

Crane, Patricia J. (2002.)
Ordering From the Cosmic Kitchen:
Essential Guide to Powerful, Nourishing Affirmations.
Bonsall, CA. Crane's Nest.

Dalconzo, Joseph Hu (2002)
Self-mastery: A journey home to your ... Self!
Forked River, NJ. Holistic Learning Centers

Fox, Emmet – "The Mental Equivalent: The Secret of Demonstration"
Publisher: Merchant Books

Gaiwan, Shakti.
Creative Visualization.
New World Library, Nataraj; 25th anniversary edition,
September 19, 2002

Gilbert, Daniel. (2005).
Stumbling on Happiness.
New York, NY. Vintage

Gilligan, Stephen. (1997).
Courage to Love: Principles and
Practices of Self-Relations Psychotherapy.
New York, NY. W.W. Norton &Company

Goleman, Daniel. (1995).
Emotional Intelligence: Why it can matter more than IQ. New York,
NY: Bantam Dell

Grant, Dr. Toni – Being a Woman: Fulfilling Your Femininity and
Finding Love
Publisher: Random House; 1st edition (February 12, 1988)

Hay, Louise L.
(1982.) Heal Your Body. Carlsbad, CA. Hay House, Inc.
(1984.) You Can Heal Your Life. Carlsbad, CA. Hay House, Inc.
(2002.) You Can Heal Your Life Companion Book. Carlsbad, CA. Hay
House, Inc.
(1991.) Power Is Within You. Carlsbad, CA. Hay House, Inc.

Holmes, Ernest – "The Science of Mind: The Complete Edition"
Publisher: Tarcher; Box Leather Deluxe edition

"Inspirational Quotations by Alan Cohen."
alancohen.com. N.p., n.d. Web. 13 Mar. 2011.

Jeffers, Susan – Feel the Fear and Do It Anyway
Publisher: Ballantine Books

Landrum, Gene. (2005).
Superman Syndrome: You Are What You Believe.
Lincoln, NE. iUniverse

Lesser, Elizabeth.
Broken Open.
N.p.: Random House, 2005. Print

Lipton, Bruce H., Ph.D. (2005.)
Biology of Belief: Unleashing the Power of Consciousness,
Matter & Miracles. Carlsbad, CA.
Hay House, Inc.194

Mandino, Og. (1977)
The Greatest Miracle in the World.
New York,NY: Bantam Books.

Millman, Dan.
Life You Were Born To Live. Tiburon, CA:
HJ Kramer Inc, 1993. Print.

Moat, Richard. Moativational Medicine ™

Morrissey, Mary. N.p.: n.p., 2009
Life Solutions at Work, LLC. Print.

Neill, Michael. (2006).
You Can Have What You Want: Proven Strategies for Inner and
Outer Success.
Hay House

Schucman, Helen – A Course in Miracles: Only Complete Edition
Publisher: Foundation for Inner Peace

Tolle, Eckhart. (1999.)
The Power of Now: A Guide to Spiritual Enlightenment. Novato, CA.
New World Library.
A New Earth: awakening to Your Life's Purpose.
N.p.: Plume, 2008. Print.

Trismegistus, Hermes – "The Kybalion: A Study of The Hermetic Philosophy of Ancient Egypt and Greece by Three Initiates"
Publisher: The Yogi Publication Society Masonic Temple – An unabridged edition of the 1908 printing

Truman, Karol.
Feelings Buried Alive Never Die. Las Vegas, NV:
Olympus Distributing, 1991. Print.

Virtue, Doreen
Assertiveness for Earth Angels: How to Be Loving Instead of "Too Nice"
Hay House, Inc., November 4, 2014

Wolinsky, Stephen. (1991).
Trances People Live: Healing Approaches In Quantum Psychology.
Falls Village, CT. !e Bramble Company

Williamson, Marianne. (2009).
Age of Miracles: Embracing the New Midlife.
Carlsbad, CA. Hay House

❦ A Call for Authors

Most people have a story that needs to be shared. Could you be one of the contributing authors to be featured in an upcoming compilation book? As a result of becoming a Published Author, some of the Visionary Insight Press contributors are now writing and speaking around the world.

Visionary Insight Press is leading the industry in compilation book publishing and represent some of today's most inspirational teachers, healers and spiritual leaders.

Their commitment is to assist this planet we call "home" to be a place of kindness, peace and love. One of the ways they fulfill this promise is by assisting others with the sharing of their inspiring stories and words of wisdom.

They look forward to hearing from you.

Please visit us at
www.visionaryinsightpress.com

CPSIA information can be obtained at www.ICGtesting.com
Printed in the USA
LVOW12s0017170615

442645LV00001B/1/P